Great Murder Trials
of the Old West

Johnny D. Boggs

Library of Congress Cataloging-in-Publication Data

Boggs, Johnny D.
  Great murder trials of the Old West / Johnny D. boggs.
      p. cm.
  Includes bibliographical references and index.
  ISBN 1-55622-892-9 (alk. paper)
  1. Trials (Murder)--West (U.S.)   I. Title.
  KF221.M8 B64 2002
  345.78'02523--dc21   2002015433

© 2003, Johnny D. Boggs
All Rights Reserved

Printed in the United States of America

ISBN 1-55622-892-9
10 9 8 7 6 5 4 3 2 1
0209

All inquiries for volume purchases of this book should be addressed t
Wordware Publishing, Inc., at 2320 Los Rios Boulevard, Plano, Texas 75074
Telephone inquiries may be made by calling:

(972) 423-0090

For my former roomate Kurt Iverson,
neither a lawyer nor a criminal
(as far as I know)

Contents

Acknowledgments

Take a deep breath. OK. Here goes. I could not have written this book without help from the following:

Anne M. Allis, University of Texas at El Paso Library Special Collections; Allison Baker, Dallas Public Library; Joyce Brunken, Yankton Community Library; Carolyn Couch, Oklahoma Historical Society; Barbara Dey, Colorado Historical Society; William H. Davis and Michael E. Pilgrim, National Archives, Washington, D.C.; Brenda Dickey and LaNell Williams, Comanche County District Clerk's office, Comanche, Texas; Stef Donev of Bakersfield, California; Carol Downey, Arizona State Archives; Marilyn F. Finke, National Archives-Central Plains Region, Kansas City, Missouri; Terri M. Grant, El Paso Public Library; Becky Gray, Tulsa City-County (Oklahoma) Library; Casey Edward Greene, Rosenberg Library, Galveston, Texas; Valerie Hanson, South Dakota State Archives; Barton Hill, Victoria (Texas) Public Library; Ken Hodgson of San Angelo, Texas; Jeanette Lundquist, Deadwood (South Dakota) Public Library; Patty Mark, Rockingham Free Public Library, Bellows Falls, Vermont; Sheri Neufeld, Tucson-Pima (Arizona) Public Library; Mark Pendleton, Branigan Library, Las Cruces, New Mexico; Lyn Spenst, Denver Public Library; Thadd Turner of Deadwood, South Dakota, and Cave Creek, Arizona; and the staffs of the Oklahoma City, San Francisco, and Santa Fe public libraries and the New Mexico State Library.

A special thanks goes to Susan Corbett of Fort Worth, Texas, who handled the first round of editing before I shipped this book off to editor Ginnie Bivona and the other powers-that-be at Republic of Texas Press.

Introduction

The images of frontier justice are clear: A tall, strong lawman stepping off a Dodge City boardwalk onto a dusty street to face down some outlaw with a gun to make Kansas safe for folks like Miss Kitty and Doc Adams.... Or a quiet ex-gunman forced to strap on his nickel-plated Colt one more time to rid a Wyoming valley of heartless, murdering robber barons and make the territory safe for folks like Van Heflin and Jean Arthur. Nice stories, certainly, but Matthew Dillon only walked the streets of a CBS back lot and other film sets, and the man called Shane was a figment of novelist Jack Schaefer's imagination, George Stevens's direction, and Alan Ladd's acting.

Pure fiction. The frontier always seemed mythical, so it stands to reason that the vision we see is mostly bunk. That's what the historians tell us, and they should know. *Mano-a-mano* gunfights on empty streets rarely happened — and who could shoot straight in a smoky saloon after several shots of red-eye? — while only an idiot would give a murderous opponent the opportunity to draw first.

Think in terms of American history, though, and similar images, though certainly less Arthurian or Homeric than the traditional western scenes cited above, come to mind: Vigilantes upholding the law with a peculiar sense of justice and hemp rope in mining camps across the Rocky Mountain West.... Wild Bill Hickok, Pat Garrett, and the Earp Brothers wielding their own brand of law with revolvers, fists and badges.... Or cattlemen taking matters into their own hands when it came to dealing with horse thieves, rustlers or, sometimes, smaller ranchers.

To paraphrase many a fictional character, where there ain't no law, you make your own. Yet, eventually, the law came to Dodge City, to Texas and Wyoming, to the entire West — and it came rather quickly. Federal and state courts brought the scales of justice to Western territories and new states. Lawyers hung their shingles from Texas to Montana and Missouri to California. Judges read law books and settled cases and lawsuits. When an ominous range war threatened an honest rancher's livelihood, you can bet your boots that his or her first trip wasn't to see the closest and fastest hired gun, but rather to sit down with an attorney at law. Maybe the Nebraska pioneer never came face-to-face with Judge Judy or watched Court TV on cable, but there was law. Real law. Not just Judge Roy Bean and his Law West of the Pecos.

Hey, Judge Issac Parker did send seventy-nine convicted felons to the gallows in Fort Smith, Arkansas, and plenty of outlaws faced juries of their peers in legal proceedings. Yet whether we read fiction or nonfiction, frontier justice seldom conveys images of barristers and courtrooms.

The idea for this book began in the late 1990s while researching a trilogy of historical novels I planned on writing regarding murder trials in the West (my *Guns and Gavel* series with Signet-Dutton). The eight trials included here aren't part of that fictional series because in these cases, I guess, truth *is* stranger than fiction. What follows is a sampling of murder trials in the Wild West — legal trials, civilian or military, not miner's courts or vigilante justice, although I do touch upon the miner's court in the Jack McCall case. Some of the defendants, such as John Wesley Hardin, and some victims, such as Wild Bill Hickok, are well known even today. Many cases have been overlooked by history, but each case turned out to become, to varying degrees, a media sensation in its time.

So some things have not changed over the past hundred-plus years. The public and the press still love a good murder trial.

Johnny D. Boggs

Santa Fe, New Mexico

"I am ready to die"

Military Trial of the Modoc Indians

⟨⟨————————————————————⟩⟩

Fort Klamath, Oregon, 1873

Prelude

Like many frontier conflicts between Indians and the newer Americans, the Modoc War was a fight for land.

White settlers began pouring into southern Oregon and northern California during the Gold Rush of the 1840s, and many became fascinated with the Lost River Valley and Tule Lake. Along the Oregon-California border, the area, while harsh (it's home today to Lava Beds National Monument), had much to offer. That's why the Modoc Indians called it home.

The first inhabitants of the region appeared sometime between 7000 and 5500 B.C. With the end of the volcanic activity in the 1400s, the ancestors of the Modocs, and their neighbors the Klamaths, began settling in the area. Ethnologists believe the Modocs and Klamaths were originally one people, but probably around the time of the American Revolution, the tribe split into two factions. The range of Modocs and Klamaths proved extensive, with the Modocs stretching five thousand square miles. Jeff Riddle, whose mother was a Modoc, described the Modocs' home:

"They hunted the deer, antelope, and bear on the hills and mountains that hemmed in Tule Lake. They shot the ducks and geese with their bows and reed arrows and caught fish in Lost River. The women gathered roots, cammus, and wocus for winter use. They lived in peace and harmony with all the tribes that joined them from all sides. The other tribes were the P[a]iute Indians, east; Pit Rivers, south; Shastas, west; and the Klamath Indians on the north."[1]

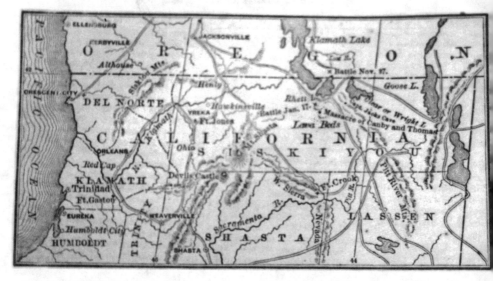

A *Harper's Weekly* map detailing the area of the Modoc War. (Author's Collection)

With increased white travel, the Modocs began trading with the newcomers, and early relationships between the two vastly different cultures were predominantly friendly. Whites, however, wanted more land for farming and ranching; the Modocs liked things as they were so they could hunt, fish, and travel. On October 9, 1864, at Council Grove, about a mile north of Klamath Agency, Oregon, Modocs, Klamaths, and a few Paiutes signed a treaty ceding all land claimed by those tribes in return for a portion of land along Upper and Middle Klamath Lakes, $8,000 in supplies for the first five years, $5,000 for the next five years, and $3,000 for the final five years after ratification of the treaty. The federal government would help build schools, shops, and mills so the Indians could assimilate into American culture.

Not every Indian was happy with the treaty, and with good reason. The Modocs and Paiutes were allowed to keep none of their traditional territory. Not only that, Modoc-Klamath relations had become tenuous at best, and now the Modocs were being forced to settle on a reservation carved out of Klamath land.

One of the more vocal objectors on the Modoc side was a young leader named Keintpoos, better known today and then as Captain Jack (the nickname was given him by Judge Elisha Steele, who thought Keintpoos looked like a miner he knew). Born around 1840, Captain Jack had advocated peace with the whites despite the death of his father, killed by settlers in an 1846 massacre.

"Capt. Jack is about 40 years old," the *Bellows Falls Times* reported in 1873. "He is five feet eight inches high, and compactly built. He has a large and well formed face, full of individuality. Although dressed in old clothes, he looks every inch a chief.... Spectators peer into Capt. Jack's face with eager interest, but he heeds them not. He is still as a statue."[2]

Like many Modocs, Captain Jack despised living with the Klamaths, and he took exception when the reservation agent backed another Modoc, Old Schonchin, to be the leader of the tribe. In 1865 Captain Jack led some of his people off the

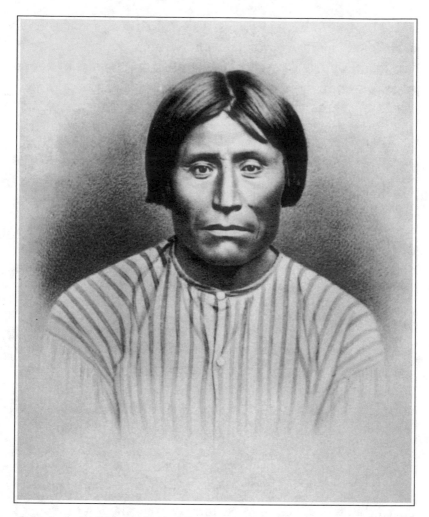

Captain Jack of the Modoc Indians was one of the principals put on trial at Fort Klamath, Oregon. (National Archives)

reservation and returned to the Lost River area to find settlers already building homesteads on Modoc land, even though the treaty had not been ratified.

Although the Modocs remained peaceful — Captain Jack often traded and drank in the town of Yreka — settlers remained uneasy. Captain Jack wasn't totally against a reservation, but he wanted a reservation for his people on traditional Modoc land. The Indian Bureau discussed the possibility of a Modoc reserve on Lost River, but ranchers objected to losing any grazing land. Settlers just wanted the Indians gone, but years passed with no new reservation and no military forcing the Modocs out of Lost River.

On April 3, 1872, Major Elmer Otis of the First Cavalry met with Captain Jack at "the Gap" on Lost River, along with J. N. High, subagent of the Klamath agency, and Ivan Applegate, commissary at Yainax station.

Major Otis informed Captain Jack that settlers complain that his band frighten women and children at their homes during the absence of the men, by going about armed and demanding food; that the Modocs have stolen cattle and hay for their ponies; have broken down fences and turned their animals in to graze, or have trampled down the grass in hay-fields, while in the pursuit of game; that these acts are charged as committed during the past winter, and still continued.

Captain Jack was warned that he must restrain or punish his men, or the whites would do it. He was reminded that the country in which he lives does not belong to his tribe, having been ceded by the Klamath treaty, which the Modocs signed; that his band were only suffered to remain where they are until the President can determine the propriety of giving them a suitable portion of land to live on apart from the Klamaths, and he was warned that he must control his men thoroughly and prevent their further molesting the settlers, and that troops would, for the present, be kept in the neighborhood to secure their quiet and good order.

Major Otis demanded of Captain Jack that he keep his Indians apart from the settlers, except when they desired to work; that when in need of food they should go to Camp Warner for supplies, but under no circumstances go armed among the settlers to demand food or to steal it.

Captain Jack at first denied these charges, and throughout the talk evaded, as far as possible, direct answers to specific charges against his band. He endeavored to convey the impression that if these thefts had been committed at all, they were the acts of the Klamaths (to which tribe the Modocs are hostile) or of other Indians, and that his own disposition and that of his tribe was friendly.[3]

Major Otis based his evidence on interviews with several settlers, although one man, Henry Miller, testified "that the Indians are not more insolent to whites than whites are to whites."[4]

As negotiations dragged on, a war grew more likely.

On November 29, 1872, T. B. Odeneal, Indian superintendent for Oregon, sent about forty troopers with the First Cavalry, commanded by Major James Jackson, to Captain Jack's camp on Lost River to take the Indians back to Klamath. Odeneal did this without the knowledge of General Edward R. S. Canby, in command of the Department of the Columbia.

Captain Jack agreed to go, with misgivings. He told Jackson: "I will take all my people with me, but I do not place any confidence in anything you white people tell me. You see you come here to my camp when it is dark. You scare me and all my people when you do that. I won't run from you. Come up to me like men, when you want to see or talk with me."[5]

The soldiers began disarming the Modocs; however, one Indian, Scarfaced Charley, laid his rifle on a pile of confiscated weapons but kept his pistol. Lieutenant Frazier Boutelle cursed the Indian and demanded that he be disarmed. Both men drew their weapons and fired, although neither drew blood, and when Scarfaced Charley reached for his rifle on the pile, others followed his example. More soldiers and Indians began firing, and by the time the army had retreated — with one man dead and seven wounded — the Modocs were fleeing to the Lava Beds, and the shooting war had begun.

Other Modocs, including Curley-Headed Doctor and Hooker Jim, soon joined Captain Jack's band, having killed fourteen settlers along their way. Captain Jack still wanted to negotiate a peaceful solution with the whites, but other Modocs were against that, believing they would be executed while Captain Jack, usually popular with the whites, would be freed.

More soldiers arrived in January, but the Modocs had the advantage of knowing their homeland. On January 13, 1873, the little band drove back the army, but more than three hundred regulars and volunteers from Oregon and California arrived three days later. Under the command of Lieutenant Colonel Frank Wheaton, the new troops assaulted the Modoc stronghold on January 17 — or tried to, anyway. Wheaton had to withdraw while the Modocs suffered no dead and only a few minor injuries.

So the federal government decided to try peaceful negotiations, and the War Department sent Canby to replace Wheaton.

Edward Richard Sprigg Canby was born at Platt's Landing, Kentucky, on November 9, 1817. After graduating from West

General Edward Canby was assassinated by Modoc Indians during what was supposed to have been peace negotiations between the Modocs and government officials. (National Archives)

Point in 1835, he served in the Seminole and Mexican wars. When the Civil War broke out, Canby, then stationed out west at Fort Defiance, was made commander of the Department of New Mexico, where he helped repel invading Confederates in 1862. In 1864 he was promoted to major general and given command of the Military Division of West Mississippi, accepting the surrender of General Kirby Smith on May 26, 1865. After the war, Canby was given a permanent rank of brigadier general. He took command of the Department of the Columbia in 1870.

Canby became part of a peace commission that also included Alfred B. Meacham, the Modocs' former agent in Oregon; Methodist preacher Eleazar Thomas of California; and Klamath reservation subagent L. S. Dyar. Canby reported his findings to General William T. Sherman by telegraph on January 30.

I am satisfied that hostilities with the Modocs would have resulted under any circumstances from the enforcement of the Commissioner's order to place them on the reservation. New facts show very clearly that they were determined to resist, and had made preparations to do so. If the arrangements for their removal had been properly carried out, the lives of the settlers who were murdered by them might have been saved, but hostilities would still have resulted, and their blows would have fallen elsewhere and alter; on the approach of a force too large to resist they would have betaken themselves to the mountains, or to their caves, and kept up the war from those points. Since the commencement they have twice attacked trains, evidently for the purpose of securing ammunition for carrying on the war.

I have been very solicitous that these Indians should be fairly treated, and have repeatedly used military force, lest they might be wronged, until their claims or pretensions were decided by proper authority. That having been done, I think they should not be treated as any other criminals, and that there will be no peace in that part of the frontier until they are subdued and punished.

Colonel [Alvan C.] Gillem acknowledges receipt of instructions of this morning, and asks if Captain Jack shall be notified that he will not be molested if he remains quiet. If not inconsistent with the President's desire, I propose to instruct him to hold communication with Captain Jack, to prevent his getting supplies of any kind, and to treat as enemies any of his party that may be found in the settlements without proper authority, but to make no aggressive movement until further notice.[6]

As the peace commission continued to negotiate, Canby considered a military alternative. "Time is becoming of the greatest importance," he reported to Sherman on March 16, "as the melting of the snow will soon enable them to live in the mountains. This will greatly increase the difficulties we have to contend with, as they will then break up into small parties, and can more readily make their escape than from their present location."[7]

A week later Canby and Gillem met with Captain Jack. Meanwhile, Canby had his forces moving in closer. Canby described Captain Jack as being under "duress."

Undoubtedly. The war faction of the Modocs began to fear that Captain Jack would betray his own people, sell them out as the other Modoc leaders, as well as Captain Jack, had done when they signed the treaty in 1864. Kill the leader of the soldiers, war proponents such as Black Jim argued, and the army would leave the Modocs alone. They began to press Captain Jack and Schonchin to murder Meacham and Canby, and the latter agreed.

"You are head chief," Black Jim told Captain Jack. "Promise us that you will kill Canby next time you meet him." Captain Jack remained adamant. "I cannot and will not do it," he said, prompting Hooker Jim's threat: "You will kill Canby or be killed yourself. You are not safe anyplace. You will kill or be killed by your own men."[8]

Reluctantly, Captain Jack agreed to murder Canby. On Good Friday, April 11, Captain Jack and Modocs Hooker Jim, Schonchin John, Ellen's Man (killed in a later battle), Black Jim, and Shacknasty Jim met with the peace commission, along with Modocs Boston Charley and Bogus Charley, who were there as interpreters, under a flag of truce near Siskiyou, California. Frank Riddle and his wife, Winema (called Toby), both of whom had helped during the negotiations, also accompanied the commissioners. Winema, who was Captain Jack's cousin, had warned Canby that she expected treachery, but Canby ignored her.

Canby gave each Modoc a cigar, which they lit from a sagebrush fire they had started to keep warm. Canby and Meacham spoke first, followed by a short address from Thomas, after which Captain Jack again asked that the Modocs be given a reservation in their country. The situation grew tense, and Meacham urged Canby to agree with Captain Jack's demands to send the soldiers away.

Too late.

At 11:48 a.m., Captain Jack drew a revolver that had been hidden underneath his coat and shot Canby in the face. Somehow, the general made it several yards out of the tent before he was brought down and swarmed upon, stabbed, and shot again. It didn't matter. The first shot was mortal.

Boston Charley gunned down Eleazar Thomas, and Meacham tried to run backward while fumbling for his derringer. A bullet tore through his whiskers, and other Modocs fired at him, and he stumbled and fell. A bullet ricocheted off a rock and hit his forehead, and he lay still, stunned. Thinking Meacham dead, the Modocs stripped him while others made sure of the fate of Thomas and Canby. Dyar and Riddle escaped during the melee, and Winema, who had been knocked down by a Modoc when the attack began, screamed that soldiers were coming.

Captain Jack and the Modoc attackers ran.

In his report to Washington, Colonel Alvan Gillem noted: "Convinced that treachery was intended, I sent for Assistant Surgeon Coburiss, who volunteered to take a note to General Canby. I could not send a verbal message, as many of the Indians understand English. I had written but a few words when shots were heard, and officers from the signal-station brought me information that General Canby and the peace commissioners had been murdered. The troops were under arms at once and advanced. I found the bodies of General Canby and the Rev. Doctor Thomas about seventy yards from the tent. Mr. Meacham was near, severely, if not mortally, wounded; all were stripped. Mr. Dyar, one of the commissioners, escaped unhurt, having a small pistol which he drew on his pursuer."[9]

Condemnation came swiftly, both in the army and in the media. General Sherman wrote to General J. M. Schofield, who commanded the military division out of San Francisco:

"The president now sanctions the most severe punishment of the Modocs, and I hope to hear that they have met the doom they so richly have earned by their insolence and perfidy."[10]

In Vermont, the *Bellows Falls Times* noted:

The treachery and murders by the Modoc Indians forms the prominent event of the week, and creates much indignation throughout the country. The government is taking decisive measures, and the result will be the total annihilation of the power of that tribe to do further mischief. And so it ought to be. It is most probable that the government have been too lenient with them already. The law of kindness does not prevail with them. They have assassinated those who were and have long been their best friends, and there appears to be no appreciation of kindness among them. They are not only untutored, but are wild and refused to be tutored, and are as insane demons, and the strong arm of the nation is the only resource left to manage them.[11]

Harper's Weekly noted:

Once more the untamable fury of the savage blood has been illustrated in the murder of the Peace Commissioners, and like wild beasts granted a temporary opportunity of mischief, the Modocs, thoughtless of the consequences, threw themselves on their victims. They had probably no restraint over their fierce impulse of revenge. They were incapable of seeing that CANBY and THOMAS were their truest friends. They thirsted for their blood like tigers....[12]

Inside the May 3, 1873 edition of *Harper's Weekly*, an artist graphically illustrates the murders of General Canby and the Reverend Doctor Thomas. (Author's Collection)

Yet *Harper's Weekly* did not preach genocide.

> Their murderers should be punished as they deserve. But the innocent should not be confounded with the guilty. Nor is it the custom of our people to encourage the cry of extermination, or to rush into excesses of severity even in the moment of an all-engrossing passion.[13]

Sherman wanted to see the Modocs stand trial, recommending a general court-martial for Captain Jack, Schonchin, and the others, citing their violation of military law by attacking mostly unarmed parties under a flag of truce. Others should be indicted for murder, he said, by Oregon's and California's civil courts, and the rest of the tribe exiled east to join a tribe that could be easily guarded such as the Winnebagos of Lake Superior. "Thus the tribe of Modocs would disappear, and the example would be salutary in dealing with other Indians similarly disposed and similarly situated."[14]

Holding Indians accountable under white law was not a new idea to Sherman. Two years earlier he had been responsible for putting Kiowa Indians Satanta and Big Tree on trial for murder in Jacksboro, Texas, after a hundred warriors ambushed and killed seven teamsters on Salt Creek Prairie during a raid. The Texas jury quickly convicted the two Indians, who were sentenced to hang, but, bowing to political pressure, the death sentence was commuted to life imprisonment at the state penitentiary in Huntsville.[15]

First, however, the Modocs had to be caught, and the army struggled with flushing the Indians out of their strongholds in the Lava Beds. Even Warm Springs Apaches brought in as trackers couldn't end the war. "In more than one instance the Modoc has been known to have two or more Spencer rifles, enabling him to keep up a rapid fire from his natural, or artificial breastwork — rock surface ground, in many places torn up by volcanic actions, which form crevices, and these are adaptable to purposes of hiding or for points of defence," the *Bellows Falls Times* noted after one battle left a reported nineteen soldiers killed and twenty-three wounded.[16]

The undoing of the Modocs came from within. Hooker Jim didn't care much for Captain Jack's strategy and eventually left him, surrendering to the army and agreeing to help track down the renegade Modocs in exchange for amnesty. On June 1, Captain Jack was captured.

The Modoc stronghold as depicted on the May 3, 1873 cover of *Harper's Weekly*. (Author's Collection)

At half-past ten o'clock this morning the Warm Spring scouts struck a trail, and after a brief search the Modocs were discovered. Col. Perry surrounded the Indian retreat. His men were bound to fight. Suddenly a Modoc shot out from the rocks with a white flag. He met a Warm Spring, and said Captain Jack wanted to surrender. Three scouts were sent out to meet Captain Jack. He came out cautiously, glanced about him a moment, and then, as if giving up all hopes, came forward and held out his hand to his visitors. Then two of his warriors, five squaws and seven children darted forth and joined him in the surrender.[17]

The worn-out leader gave his rifle to an officer and said: "Jack's legs gave out. I am ready to die."[18]

Trial

After debating the legality of trying the Modocs, United States Attorney General George H. Williams ruled in mid-June that a military commission could try the accused Indians, and the War Department ordered Captain Jack and five others to stand trial at Fort Klamath, Oregon. The new army commander in the region, General Jefferson C. Davis, had wanted them summarily executed.

The military post had been established in September 1863, eight miles north of Upper Klamath Lake and about five miles from the Klamath Indian Agency. One correspondent offered a travel writer's portrait of the fort:

Klamath is justly reputed one of the prettiest and most attractive military stations on the Pacific slope, and certainly is a grand place for the closing scenes in the Modoc drama. The post proper occupies a site on a broad, green meadow, that is belted by...pines, which are in turn encompassed, or nearly so, by snowy peaks of the Cascade Range — a carpet of green with a forest for a border, and a fringe of mountains; whitened cottages, barracks and barns and many tents relieving any tendency for sameness in the scene, and forming pleasant contrasts; the whole constituting a landscape beautiful to behold, harmonious in its various phases and impressive in its character. Such is Fort Klamath.[19]

Detailed for the tribunal were Lieutenant Colonel Washington L. Elliott, First Cavalry, the senior member of the board who had joined the army on May 27, 1846; Captain John Mendenhall, Fourth Artillery, an 1851 graduate of West Point; Captain Henry C. Hasbrouck, Fourth Artillery, an 1861 West Point graduate who had also briefly taught at the Academy; Captain Robert Pollock, Twenty-first Infantry, a former volunteer who had been commissioned in the regular army after the Civil War, of whom was said "San Francisco is largely indebted to him for the organization of that crack military company, the National Guard"[20]; and Second Lieutenant George W. Kingsbury, Twelfth Infantry, who survived serious wounds in the Civil War and later was appointed to the regular army. A resident of Bellows Falls, Vermont, Kingsbury also wrote several articles for his hometown newspaper, the *Bellows Falls Times*, during the Modoc War that are among the best sources of material for that period.

Major H. P. Curtis served as judge advocate. Curtis joined the Fifty Massachusetts Cavalry in January 1862 and fought with the Army of the Potomac throughout the Civil War. Afterward, he was promoted to major and made the army's judge advocate. "He has entered upon his work with a hearty good will," the *San Francisco Daily Morning Call* reported. "There cannot be convictions without evidence — and evidence in the Peace Commission tragedy, is a scarce article."[21]

The commission met first on July 1 at Fort Klamath, but Curtis informed the panel that he was not prepared to proceed so the court was adjourned until 10 a.m. July 5. The prisoners were kept in the post guardhouse, a white thirty-by-forty-foot building. A correspondent for the *San Francisco Daily Morning Call* described the conditions of the prisoners, each allowed to smoke one pipe of tobacco a day: "The prisoners look bad. They huddle together and make no noise that can be heard two feet from the cell doors.... Every captive wore a dejected air, and some looked as if death in any form would be welcomed as a measure of relieve."[22]

The prisoners could hear little of what was going on outside the guardhouse and could see nothing. Perhaps that was a good thing. The gallows were being constructed during the trial — even before a verdict and sentence were handed down.

When court reconvened, Frank Riddle and his wife were employed as interpreters, receiving $10 a day, and E. S. Belden was sworn in to transcribe the testimony. Curtis then asked the prisoners if they wanted counsel. They answered no; they hadn't been able to find anyone to represent them.

So the trial began with the reading of the charges against Captain Jack, Schonchin, Boston Charley, Black Jim, Barncho (alias One-Eyed Jim), and Sloluck (alias Cok). They were charged with the murder of Canby and Thomas and assault with intent to kill Meacham and Dyar. Each defendant pleaded not guilty, and Frank Riddle was called to testify.

Riddle described Captain Jack as chief and Schonchin as subchief. Black Jim was a watchman, Boston Charley a "high private," and the latter two "not anything."[23] He covered his visits to the Lava Beds as well as his wife's warnings, which went unheeded by Canby and others. "[M]y woman went and took hold of Mr. Meacham and told him not to go; and held on to him and cried," Riddle said. "She said 'Meacham, don't you go!' — I heard her say so myself — 'for they might kill you to-day; they may kill all of you to-day'; and Dr. Thomas, he came up and told me that I ought to put my trust in God; that God Almighty would not let any such body of men be hurt that was on as good a mission as that. I told him at the time that he might trust in God, but that I didn't trust any in them Indians."[24]

Riddle went on to relate the speeches made by the commission at the peace tent. Then Captain Jack "stepped back and came right up in front of General Canby, and said, in Indian, 'All ready boys' — At we — that is, 'All ready,' and the cap bursted [his pistol misfired], and before you could crack your finger he fired."

Q: You saw this?

A: Yes, sir; and after the cap bursted, before you could crack your finger, he fired and struck General Canby under the eye, and the ball came out here [showing — in the neck, under the chin]. I jumped and ran then, and never stopped to look back any more. I saw General Canby fall over, and I expected he was killed, and I jumped and ran with all my might. I never looked back but once, and when I looked back Mr. Meacham was down and my woman was down, and there was an Indian standing over Mr. Meacham and another Indian standing over her, and some two or three coming up to Mr. Meacham. Mr. Meacham was sort of lying down this way [showing] and had one of his hands sticking out.

Q: You saw General Canby fall, you say?

A: Yes, sir.

Q: Did he continue to lie where he fell?

A: He was not when they found him; he was about thirty or forty yards from there. I did not see him get up.

After Riddle finished testifying for the judge advocate, the Modoc prisoners — still without representation — were asked if they wanted to cross-examine the witness. They declined.

The court asked a few more questions for explanation, the most important of which asked the witness if he saw only Captain Jack shoot his weapon. Riddle answered that he also saw Schonchin fire.

Riddle's wife, who testified next, said she had been "sitting or laying down, rather pretty close, sort of between Meacham and Riddle," when Captain Jack opened fire. She then saw Schonchin fire at Meacham, and Hooker Jim fire at Dyar while chasing him. Boston Charley, she said, shot Thomas first.

Once the judge advocate finished direct examination, the defendants again declined to cross-examine, and agent Dyar took the stand.

Dyar explained how Boston Charley had told the commissioners that Captain Jack had agreed to meet them, unarmed (not all of the whites obeyed that requirement either, but Dyar omitted this oversight). He also described the attack and how he escaped. After the Modocs declined to question him, court was adjourned until July 7.

The first witness called when court reconvened was Shacknasty Jim, testifying for the prosecution. In quick testimony he said how, on the night before the attack, he heard Captain Jack and Schonchin talk of killing the peace commissioners, and later reiterated what previous witnesses had seen during the attack. Another Modoc, Steamboat Frank, said more of the same when he was called to the stand. After Dyar was recalled to clarify minor points, other Modocs took the stand against the defendants.

Bogus Charley admitted he didn't like Captain Jack, after quarreling with him at Dry Lake. Present at the attack, he said he didn't know the Modocs planned on killing the commissioners on that particular day but had heard Captain Jack and Schonchin discussing their plans earlier.

Hooker Jim, who had been responsible for the deaths of many settlers on his way to join the Modoc holdouts and then helped betray Captain Jack, took the stand, conveniently omitting that Hooker Jim had been the one who told Captain Jack he would die if he didn't kill Canby. Granted amnesty, he admitted that he had agreed to kill one of the peace commissioners if he could and had chased and shot at Dyar.

Another Modoc, Whim (or William), said he had told Toby Riddle that the commissioners would be killed at the meeting.

Captain Jack and his co-defendants never asked any questions.

The day's final witness was Meacham, who covered much ground already traversed by previous witnesses. He also repeated the speech Thomas gave after Canby had spoken on that fateful morning.

> Toby, tell these people that I think the Great Spirit
> put it into the heart of the President to send us here. I
> have known General Canby for fourteen years; I have

known Mr. [Dyar] for a few years, and Mr. Meacham for eighteen years; and I know their hearts, and I know they are all your friends; and I know my own heart and I believe that God sees us, what we do; that he wishes us all to be at peace; that no more blood should be shed.

Again, the murders were described, along with Meacham's own injuries. No Modoc asked the witness anything.

The following day Fourth Artillery Lieutenant H. R. Anderson gave routine testimony — he had not seen the murders — and assistant surgeon Henry C. McEldery described the victims. Asked if Canby was dead, McEldery gave a not quite so medical reply: "Yes, sir; he was quite dead when I saw him."

Curtis asked the surgeon to be a little more specific.

"He had been entirely stripped of every article of clothing," McEldery said. "He had three wounds on his body, and several abrasions of the face. One of the wounds, apparently made by a ball, was about at the inner canthus of the left eye. The edges of that wound were depressed, as if the ball had entered there."

Thomas, McEldery said, had been shot several times, with a bullet to the heart causing his death.

As usual, the Modocs didn't bother asking any questions, and the judge advocate rested his case.

First to testify for the defense was Scarfaced Charley, who, prompted by two questions from Captain Jack, gave a rambling account of the Modoc War and blamed the Klamath Indians and their chief, David Allen, for the affair — not that it offered much of a defense for the killing of Thomas and Canby.

Questioned by the court, however, Scarfaced Charley named the defendants who met with the peace commission on the day of the murders. A Modoc named Dave also criticized David Allen (derisively called Allen David by the Modocs) and the Klamaths. Nor did One-Eyed Mose, in his brief testimony, offer any evidence that could lead to an acquittal. Finally, Captain Jack made a statement, interpreted by one of the Riddles, on his own behalf.

"I never accused any white man of being mean and bad," he said. "I always thought them my friends, and when I went to any one and asked him for a pass, he would always give it to me; all gave me passes, and told those people who had to pass through my country that I was a good Indian, and had never disturbed anybody."

He didn't object to whites passing through Modoc land or even living in his country, and the only people who thought him bad were the Klamaths.

"I hardly know how to talk here," he said later. "I don't know how white people talk in such a place as this; but I will do the best I can."

Curtis encouraged him. "Talk exactly as if you were at home, in a council."

"I have always told white men when they came to my country, that if they wanted a home to live there they could have it; and I never asked them for any pay for living there as my people lived. I liked to have them come there and live. I liked to be with white people. I didn't know anything about the war — when it was going to commence. Major Jackson came down there and commenced on me while I was in bed asleep."

Jackson, Captain Jack said, was to blame for the November attack that precipitated the entire affair. He went on to say that a civilian named Nate Berwick told him the commissioners planned on murdering the Modocs at the council. He also lashed out at Hooker Jim and others.

"Your chief makes his men mind him and listen to him, and they do listen to what he tells them, and they believe him; but my people won't. My men would not listen to me. They wanted to fight. I told them not to fight. I wanted to talk and make peace and live right; but my men would not listen to me...

"Hooker Jim was the one that agitated the fighting; that wanted to fight all of the time. I sat over to one side with my few men and did not say anything about fighting. Now I have to bear the blame for him and the rest of them."

Schonchin made a brief statement but didn't offer any defense. None of the other accused spoke, and court was adjourned until the next day, when Captain Jack continued his statement.

> The four scouts have told you they didn't know anything about the murder of General Canby; and they advocated the murder of General Canby with me. The Indians that told that the talk took place in my house about the murder of General Canby, lie. It was their own house it took place in....I would like to know why Hooker Jim could not tell who he wanted to kill when he went out there. He says he went there to kill a man; but he would not tell the man he wanted to kill. Meacham was the man that he wanted to kill. Them four scouts knew all about it; and they were in our councils when we were holding councils, and they all wanted to kill the peace commissioners; they all advised me to do it....

Another thing that made me afraid to meet the commissioners, the Indians lied to me and told me that Dr. Thomas and the other peace commissioners had pistols with them, and wanted to kill us. I told them that I didn't see any pistols with anybody, and they surely must have lied. I told them that I did not want to have any trouble with the peace commissioners; that I did not want to kill them. Hooker Jim, he said that he wanted to kill Meacham, and we must do it. That is all I have to say.

The trial was, for all intent and purpose, over, and the verdict came quickly. Each defendant was found guilty of all charges and specifications and sentenced to death by hanging. Execution date was set for October 3.

Aftermath

The verdict and sentence were met with approval throughout Oregon, California, and most of the United States. Major Curtis, however, requested leniency for Barncho and Sloluck. "The others were all involved deeply in the plot to murder, consulted about it with each other and acted as ringleaders, I have no doubt," he wrote the attorney general. "Barncho and Sloluck, however, I regard as common soldiers, who obeyed orders in being present, or rather within hail, and whom it will be an unnecessary outlay of national vengeance to put to death."[25]

The recommendation was granted, and Barncho and Sloluck were given life sentences at Alcatraz, but the two prisoners would not be informed of the commutation just yet.

There was sympathy for the condemned Modocs, though, among the Society of Friends, better known as Quakers. Lewis Palmer, a Quaker from Concordville, Pennsylvania, wrote President Grant on September 11, 1873. "I do not claim to be a saint," he wrote, "but if rightly knowing my own mind, I have a strong desire for the advancement of truth and practical righteousness." He continued:

I presume thou hast received many letters in relation to the Modocs, and I do not wish to be in any way troublesome, but as I sat in meeting this morning the subject of those prisoners arose before my mind, and it seemed to impress me so forcibly that I believe it to be right to lay the case before thee, hoping thy judgment in the matter (be it what it may) will be for the very best.

It appeared to me that the Government that had shown so much advancement in Christian charity in its treatment of those lately in rebellion against it should not now be stained with the blood of a few miserable savages; poor, ignorant, and deluded, yet, withal, men and brothers in the sight of the Infinite Creator of us all. And the proposition came before me which I will state, in a spirit of love, for thy consideration.

It is that those prisoners may be sent to some island or place of security for the rest of their lives, with or without some of the rest of their tribe, and that some one or more be sent with them to have charge over them; that endeavors be used to enlighten them in the better way of life, and awaken in their hearts that sense of truth and right which will lead them into a condemnation of their previous course.

Now, though I have a good home, am surrounded with a family whom I love, and have no desire for preferment in political affairs, yet should there be no one more suitable, nor willing, to undertake the task, my name is at thy command, for, as undesirable to me as is the undertaking, I would much rather do it than to see the Christian name and power of this beloved nation lowered in the sight of God and man.

Palmer's plea fell on deaf ears. The rest of the convicted Modocs would hang.

On Friday, October 3, a crowd gathered at Fort Klamath to watch the execution. Attendance was mandatory for all soldiers stationed at the fort as well as the remaining Modoc prisoners. Many civilians also arrived, and Klamath Indians were allowed to watch. Reporters were stationed at the foot of the gallows, completed the day before.

At 9:30 a.m., guards marched the six shackled prisoners to the gallows. Captain Jack climbed the steps first, followed by Schonchin, Boston Charley, and Black Jim. Still unaware of their luck, Sloluck and Barncho sat on the coffins, waiting their turn to hang.

"Jack!" a settler called out from the crowd. "What would you give me to take your place?" Captain Jack replied: "Five hundred ponies and both my wives."[26]

At 9:50, the four Modocs sat on the scaffold, and execution orders were read. The post adjutant then let Barncho and Sloluck know their lives had been spared. The two men received the news "with great joy"[27] and were then marched to the front of the gallows. After a short prayer by the post chaplain, the officer of the day ordered the execution to proceed.

His assistants securely tied the condemned prisoners at the elbows, knees and feet, and after adjusting the ropes, placed the black caps over their heads and everything was ready. At a signal from the commanding officer, communicated through the officer of the day, the man in charge of the drop cut the rope and in an instant the four wretches were swinging in eternity.

Everything connected with the execution was in most perfect order and was performed in strict military precision. The drop was perfect and fearfully effective. Capt. Jack and Black Jim never moved a muscle after the fall. Schonchin and Boston Charley appeared to suffer but very little.

The bodies were allowed to hang for thirty minutes when they were cut down, put in their coffins and buried...in close proximity to the post guard house, where the sentinel, in death as well as in life, will watch over them and take good care that they are not disturbed.[28]

But Captain Jack's body was disturbed. That night, his body was dug up and sent to Yreka for embalming. Instead of being returned, the story goes, the corpse went to Washington, D.C., where easterners paid ten cents each to see it in some freak show. Eventually the surgeon general acquired the body, by then only a skeleton, and placed it in a museum.

Sloluck and Barncho were pardoned after spending five years at Alcatraz. Barncho died six years later, while Sloluck lived until 1899. After the 1873 execution, the remaining Modoc prisoners, 153 men, women, and children (including Hooker Jim and his cronies) were sent to Indian Territory.

There they remained until 1909, when the surviving fifty-one were allowed to return to a Modoc reservation in Oregon.

Did the Modocs receive a fair trial? Transcripts from the proceedings show the court acted fairly, but the accused had no counsel and understood little English, so how just could it have been? The bigger question seems to be this: Was the Modoc War worth the price? In addition to the lives lost, the campaign cost $1 million. The land Captain Jack wanted for a Modoc reservation would have cost only $20,000.

Chapter Notes

Primary sources: *War with the Modoc Indians, 1872-1873*; 43rd Congress, 1st Session; House of Representatives Executive Document No. 122, 1874; *The Modocs and Their War* (University of Oklahoma Press, 1959) by Keith A. Murray; *Guardhouse, Gallows and Graves: The Trial and Execution of Indian Prisoners of the Modoc Indian War by the U.S. Army 1873* (Klamath County Museum, 1988) compiled by Francis S. Landrum; *Hell With the Fire Out* (Faber and Faber, 1997) by Arthur Quinn; *The Indian History of the Modoc War* (Urion Press, 1974) by Jeff C. Riddle; *Bury My Heart at Wounded Knee* (Washington Square Press, 1981) by Dee Brown; *Harper's Weekly*, May 3, 1873; and various 1873 editions of the *Bellows Falls Times* and *San Francisco Daily Morning Call*.

1. Riddle, Jeff C. *The Indian History of the Modoc War*, p. 15.
2. *Bellows Falls Times*, June 6, 1873.
3. *War with the Modoc Indians, 1872-1873*; 43rd Congress, 1st Session.
4. Ibid.
5. Riddle, pp. 44-45.
6. *War with the Modoc Indians, 1872-1873*.
7. Ibid.
8. Riddle, p. 72.

9. *War with the Modoc Indians, 1872-1873.*

10. *Bellows Falls Times*, April 18, 1873.

11. Ibid.

12. *Harper's Weekly*, May 3, 1873.

13. Ibid.

14. *War with the Modoc Indians, 1872-1873.*

15. Satanta and Big Tree would be released in August 1873. Satanta, however, was returned to Huntsville after the 1874-75 Indian uprising and killed himself in the prison in 1878. Big Tree remained free and died in Oklahoma in 1929.

16. *Bellows Falls Times*, May 2, 1873.

17. *Bellows Falls Times*, June 6, 1873.

18. Brown, Dee. *Bury My Heart at Wounded Knee*, p. 233.

19. *San Francisco Daily Morning Call*, July 1, 1873.

20. *San Francisco Daily Morning Call*, July 6, 1873.

21. Ibid.

22. *San Francisco Daily Morning Call*, July 1, 1873.

23. *War with the Modoc Indians, 1872-1873.* All testimony comes from this account, unless otherwise noted. The transcripts were also reprinted in *Guardhouse, Gallows and Graves*, compiled by Francis S. Landrum.

24. Ibid.

25. *War with the Modoc Indians, 1872-1873.*

26. Murray, Keith A. *The Modocs and Their War*, p. 303.

27. *Bellows Falls Times*, October 10, 1873.

28. *Bellows Falls Times*, October 24, 1873.

"A cowardly, treacherous desperado"

Trial of Jack McCall

«←————————————————————————————→»

Yankton, Dakota Territory, 1876-77

Prelude

More than one hundred and twenty-five years after his death, he remains the world's most famous gunfighter. His name was James Butler Hickok, but he was better known as "Wild Bill" and had become a living legend by the time he came to the Black Hills in what is now southwestern South Dakota in the summer of 1876.

Born on a La Salle County farm near Homer (now Troy Grove), Illinois, on May 27, 1837, Hickok moved west to Kansas with brother Lorenzo in the summer of 1856, four years after their father, William Alonzo Hickok, died. They came to establish a land claim, but Lorenzo returned to Illinois after a while, and James was left alone. An abolitionist, Hickok joined the Free State Army led by Senator James H. Lane, the "Grim Chieftain of Kansas," as a scout in the late 1850s, served as constable of Monticello, and worked as a teamster with the freighting and stagecoach firm of Russell, Majors and Waddell, where he developed a lifelong friendship with a young frontiersman named William F. Cody.

By all accounts he was a striking figure, standing more than six feet tall, with broad shoulders, blue-gray eyes, and shoulder-length hair and large mustache described as "tawny,"

Photo from a 1952 postcard announcing the re-enactment of Deadwood's "Trial of Jack McCall." Deadwood still celebrates the miner's court acquittal, while Yankton, site of the federal murder charge and hanging, quietly forgets its place in history.
(Author's Collection)

"perfect blond," "fine dark" and, probably correct, "auburn in hue." He dressed in fancy duds and seems to have favored Colt's 1851 .36-caliber Navy model revolvers. Most considered him mild-mannered unless provoked.

In March 1861 Hickok, recovering from some type of injury (some historians say he had been mauled by a bear), was working for Russell, Majors and Waddell at Rock Creek Stage Station in Nebraska. On July 12 a border ruffian named David McCanles and Hickok quarreled. The reasons and circumstances have been disputed since the first shot was fired, but the result was that McCanles and two companions were dead, and Hickok would soon become known as the "Prince of Pistoleers."

Hickok served in the Union army during the Civil War and killed Davis K. Tutt in a gunfight at Springfield, Missouri, after being mustered out of the army in June 1865. He spent the next two years as an army scout and saw his fame go national with the February 1867 publication of an exaggerated account of Wild Bill's exploits written by Colonel George Ward Nichols in *Harper's New Monthly Magazine*. In Kansas he worked as a deputy U.S. marshal around Fort Hays, sheriff of Ellis County, and town marshal of Abilene. His career as a lawman, however, ended after an October 5, 1871 gunfight in Abilene during which he shot Texas hardcase Phil Coe and then killed a man who rushed upon the scene. Coe died three days later, and the second man, who had been killed instantly, turned out to be Michael Williams, one of Hickok's deputies.

He gambled and even took to show business, most prominently as part of touring stage production in 1873-74 with fellow frontiersmen John "Texas Jack" Omohundro and old friend Cody, better known these days as "Buffalo Bill." The performances were generally panned by theater critics, but audiences packed the venues in New Jersey, Pennsylvania, New York, Ohio, Kentucky, Indiana, Maryland, Connecticut, Rhode Island, Massachusetts, Maine, and New Hampshire. Dissatisfied with acting and irritated that Omohundro and Cody seemed to be making fun of their accomplishments out West, Hickok left the troupe in March 1874 and returned west to the gambling halls and his element.

A writer described Hickok in *Scribner's Monthly*:

Most of the Western scouts do not amount to much. They do a great deal in the personal reminiscence way, but otherwise they are generally of the class described as "frauds." In "Wild Bill," I found a man who talked little and had done a great deal. He was about six feet two inches in height, and very powerfully built; his face was intelligent, his hair blonde, and falling in long ringlets upon his broad shoulders; his eyes, blue and pleasant, looked one straight in the face when he talked; and his lips, thick and compressed, were only partly hidden by a straw-colored mustache. His costume was a curiously blended union of the habiliments of the borderman and the drapery of the fashionable dandy. Beneath the skirts of his elaborately embroidered buckskin coat gleamed the handles of two silver-mounted revolvers, which were his constant companions. His voice was low and musical, but through its hesitation I could catch a ring of self-reliance and consciousness of strength. Yet he was the most courteous man I had ever met on the plains.[1]

On March 5, 1876, in the home of S. L. Moyer in Cheyenne, Wyoming, Hickok married circus performer Agnes Lake Thatcher, whom he had met in Abilene in 1871. After the

Wild Bill Hickok, as depicted by a *Scribner's Monthly* artist,
a year after the pistoleer's death. (Author's Collection)

couple went on a brief honeymoon in Thatcher's hometown of
Cincinnati, Hickok returned to Cheyenne and in late June left
for the boom town of Deadwood with friend Charles E. "Colorado Charlie" Utter and Utter's brother, Steve. Hickok hoped
to earn enough money gambling to send to his new bride.

Technically, Deadwood was an illegal town.

Dakota Territory had been formed in 1861, but the Fort
Laramie Treaty of 1868 designated the Black Hills as part of
the Great Sioux Indian Reservation. In 1874, however,

Lieutenant Colonel George Armstrong Custer of the Seventh Cavalry led an expedition into the Black Hills, where traces of gold and other minerals were discovered. Word quickly spread, and prospectors began to enter the reservation illegally. Although the army was instructed to remove the white miners, a group led by T. H. Russell, Charles Collins, and John Gordon arrived on December 23, 1874, and began a settlement and mining operation. By the summer of 1875, with more and more miners entering the Black Hills, the army began to realize that if the area became populated with too many whites to remove, perhaps it would speed up renegotiations with the Sioux to remove the Black Hills from their reservation. Later that summer a miner named John B. Pearson discovered gold in what became known as Deadwood Gulch. Twenty miners wintered on Deadwood Gulch. Deadwood would attract twenty-five thousand people in 1876.

Leander P. Richardson arrived in Deadwood on July 31, 1876, and described the camp of Charlie Utter and Hickok in an 1893 letter to the New York *Sun*:

[Hickok] slept in a big canvas covered wagon, rolled up in an army blanket. Every morning, just before breakfast, he used to crawl out, clad in his shirt, trousers and boots, tie his hair in a knot at the back of his head, shove his big revolver down inside the waistband of his trousers, and run like a sprinter down the gulch to the nearest saloon. In a few minutes he would come strolling back, with a cocktail or two stowed away where it would do the most good, and would complete his toilet. . . . [2]

An artist's sketch of Deadwood Gulch that appeared in the April 1877 edition of *Scribner's Monthly*. (Author's Collection)

Another early Deadwood pioneer, John S. McClintock, recalled:

In a recent write-up of Wild Bill, it is stated that in coming to Deadwood, he remarked to his friends, "Boys, I have a hunch that this is my last camp and that I will never leave it alive," and that he made the statement the evening before his death that he believed his time on earth was short. These expressions of fear have been construed by his ardent admirers as presentiment of his approaching death. Whether or not he actually did thus express himself, there can be little doubt that such premonitions of death must have been present in his mind. With thousands of people of all characters and from all directions flocking to Deadwood, this was the place where he was likely to meet the avenger.[3]

Hickok certainly had some type of premonitions, for in his last letter to his wife, dated August 1, 1876, he wrote: "If such should be we never meet again, while firing my last shot, I will gently breathe the name of my wife — Agnes — and with wishes even for my enemies I will make the plunge and try to swim to the other shore."[4]

While Charlie Utter was busy trying to establish a pony express service between Deadwood and Cheyenne, Hickok frequented the gambling tables. On August 1, he apparently had been playing poker with a group of men including a miner called Bill Sutherland. Hickok wound up busting Sutherland and then offering him spare change, about seventy-five cents, for supper or breakfast. Sutherland refused the offer and left.

About noon on August 2, Hickok entered Lewis, Nuttall and Mann's No. 10 Saloon and joined a poker game with Carl Mann, part owner of the establishment; William Massie, a former riverboat pilot, and Charlie Henry Rich, a young gambler. Rich was seated with his back to the west wall, and Hickok asked him to move. As a noted gunman, Hickok never sat with his back to a door or bar, but Rich did not wish to change seats and, perhaps, his luck. Hickok did not persist and settled into another chair.

About three o'clock Sutherland entered the No. 10 Saloon. His real name was John McCall, alias Jack McCall. About twenty-five years old, McCall is believed to have come from either Jefferson Town, Kentucky, or New Orleans. He was cross-eyed, slender, about medium height, with chestnut hair and a sandy mustache and a snub nose. Some descriptions said he also wore a goatee. "His face is one which would not recommend him to a casual observer as a man free from guilt," a reporter with the *Yankton Press and Dakotaian* observed, "while his actions made it manifest that he is possessed of a fair share of animal courage."[5]

Another newspaper correspondent editorialized:

McCall's appearance would indicate him to be a murderous villain. He is about 5 feet 8 inches in height, rather solidly built, with brown, curly hair, has a light mustache, is cross-eyed and has a malicious and sinister expression of countenance which would stamp him anywhere as being a cowardly, treacherous desperado.[6]

Weighing gold dust on the scales at the end of the bar, George Shingle stood near bartender Harry Young not far from Hickok's table. In the front of the saloon, Joseph Mitchell was putting in wainscoting. McCall walked to the scales, watched Shingle for a while, and next headed toward the rear door. Hickok could not see McCall now, and his mind was on the poker hand he had just lost to Massie. He tossed his hand on the table and said, "The old duffer, he broke me on that hand." The myth, however, persists that Hickok was holding aces and eights, which became known as the Dead Man's Hand, at the time. No one knows what he had, but it didn't win.

At that moment Jack McCall turned around, drew and cocked a pistol, and fired. He was standing about two or three feet behind Hickok. The bullet entered the back of the gun-man's head, exited near the bottom of his nose on the right cheek, and lodged in Massie's left arm just above the wrist. Hickok fell off his stool without uttering a word, dead at age thirty-nine.

Screaming, "Come on ye sons a bitches," McCall backed toward the rear door. He aimed at Shingle, who was moving to help Hickok, and pulled the trigger, but the gun misfired. He might also have fired at Mann, but the only round he got off was the one that killed Hickok. McCall ran out of the No. 10 and tried to escape or find a place to hide but was soon captured and marched back to Main Street. Talk spread of lynching the killer, but McCall was probably saved when a Mexican came into town carrying the head of an Indian. That gruesome sight must have been even more exciting than a lynching, because in the end, the miners and merchants of Deadwood decided to hold a miner's court[7] the following morning and try McCall.

At the Deadwood Theatre, William Littlebury Kuykendall was elected judge, and Isaac Brown, a saloonkeeper and mer-chant, was chosen sheriff. A local lawyer named Colonel George May was selected prosecutor, while McCall asked A. B. Chapline to defend him. Chapline, claiming sickness, could not attend, so a Judge Miller served as defense counsel. At two o'clock the miner's court began. An hour later Colorado Charlie Utter was overseeing the funeral and burial of Wild Bill.

> The body was clothed in a full suit of broad-cloth, the hair brushed back from the broad forehead, and the blood washed from the pallid cheek. Beside the

A view of the Lower End of Deadwood, which accompanied an
article titled "A Trip to the Black Hills" in *Scribner's Monthly*, April 1877.
(Author's Collection)

dead hero lay his rifle, which was buried with him.
The funeral ceremony was brief and touching, hun-
dreds of miners standing around the bier with bowed
heads and tear-dimmed eyes, — for with the better
class "Wild Bill" had been a great favorite. At the close
of the ceremony the coffin was lowered into a

new-made grave on the hill-side, — the first in Dead-wood.[8]

The jury consisted of foreman Charles Whitehead, J. J. Bump, L. D. Bookaw, J. H. Thompson, S. S. Hopkins, J. F. Cooper, Alex Travis, K. E. Towle, J. E. Thompson, L. A. Judd, Ed Burke, and John Mann.

In his memoirs published in 1917, Judge Kuykendall recalled the miner's court:

Evidence showed no provocation whatever and no motive save for a love for notoriety, coupled with a full glass of whiskey taken in a saloon opposite, from which he could see the two players and the barkeeper, who were the only persons in the place. At noon the sheriff informed me that he had carefully listed those present who were in the meeting the night before and besides the officers only five had been present at the trial. For a moment I lost faith in humanity. He said there could only be one verdict — "guilty," to which I replied that I would do the sentencing in short order and expected him to be as expeditious with the immediate hanging. He assured me he would.[9]

McCall's defense was that he killed Hickok to avenge his brother's death at the gunman's hand "at some place in Kansas."[10] Judge Kuykendall, and likely others, were aware this was a lie. Kuykendall charged the jury around sundown, McCall was confined in a cabin, and, because the theater would not be available, the verdict would be announced the following morning, pending a unanimous decision by the jury, at, ironically, the No. 10 Saloon.

Kuykendall and Brown selected fifteen deputies and had a chalk line drawn across the No. 10's floor to mark the courtroom. The saloon was packed with men the next morning when the prisoner and jury were brought in. Kuykendall recalled:

> When the prisoner was seated, his feet beat a tattoo on the floor, and his teeth were chattering. He was a pitiable object of abject fear. The outside space in the room filled with men even up to the chalk line and a pin could have been heard to drop.
>
> When the jury was in place I asked the foreman if they had agreed upon their verdict. He answered yes. "Mr. Foreman," I said, "you will pass the verdict to the clerk, who will read it." The verdict was, "We, the jury, find the defendant not guilty." McCall hurried out through the back door and was soon on a swift horse, fleeing the country.... [11]

Kuykendall, Colonel May, and many of Hickok's friends, including Utter and California Joe, were outraged. Kuykendall wrote: "The Deadwood jury, though remaining in the country, immediately dropped out of sight and hearing, and not until a few years ago did I find one of them in Deadwood, who said the jury agreed that McCall was clearly guilty and their verdict was a travesty of justice, but the cause for the verdict was the belief that the gamblers and real vicious element would run the county if their verdict were 'guilty,' one of the most absurd propositions ever advanced...." [12]

McCall fled the Black Hills for Cheyenne and Laramie. He even began to brag of his deed. The killer became an obsession with May, who began a correspondence with Hickok's widow and followed McCall to Wyoming. The cross-eyed gambler's boasting would be his undoing. Wyoming Territory was under federal jurisdiction, and when May joined McCall's audience and heard him say he had killed the great Wild Bill Hickok, May reported it to the law. On August 29, a deputy United States marshal named St. A. D. Balcombe arrested McCall.

"I made some statements while at Laramie, but they were entirely misrepresented; the newspapers published a whole lot of stuff, running me down the worst way," McCall told a reporter for the *Dakota Herald*.[13]

After hearings in Cheyenne before the U.S. Commissioner and a judge, McCall was taken to Yankton, the capital of Dakota Territory, for trial.

"The penitentiary seems to be looming up before McCall," the *Cheyenne Daily Leader* reported.[14]

Actually, it was the gallows.

Trial

McCall was held at the federal jail on Linn Street in Yankton and on October 18 was taken to the U.S. District Court House, where he was indicted for murder. Presiding at the hearing was Granville G. Bennett, assistant justice of the territory's Supreme Court. After the indictment was read, the court asked the defendant if his real name was John McCall. He said it was. McCall also told the court that he had no counsel and no funds to pay for one, so Bennett assigned Oliver Shannon and Colonel G. C. Moody as McCall's attorneys. Moody would later be replaced by General W. H. H. Beadle. Shannon immediately asked for a continuance to prepare a defense, and McCall entered a plea of not guilty. On the following day the defense requested a postponement of the trial so that four defense witnesses could be brought to Yankton. Subpoenas were issued for John Weldon, Daniel Boyd, James Lamb, and George Robertson or Robinson to testify for McCall. Prosecution witnesses summoned included George Shingle and Captain William Massie. Court was adjourned until November 27.

On November 9 McCall and cellmate Jerry McCarty, who was awaiting trial for the July 9 stabbing death of John Hinch at Gayville, about one-and-a-half miles west of Deadwood Gulch, made a break for freedom. The *Yankton Press and Dakotaian* reported:

> J. B. Robinson, the jailor, was preparing to lock up his prisoners in their cells for the night, when he was seized by McCarty, thrown upon the floor and held by the throat. McCall then came to the assistance of McCarty, pounded Robinson on the head and body until he was nearly unconscious and then took his keys away from him. The two desperadoes then broke their shackles with the round of a chair and proceeded to liberate themselves from confinement. They unlocked the door of the jail, but just as they were stepping out into open air and liberty, they were met by U.S. Marshal Burdick and James Bennett, one of his assistants, who opportunely happened along. Marshal Burdick immediately comprehended the situation and placed the business end of his revolver in unpleasant proximity to the heads of the escaping murderers, while Bennett followed suit. They took in the situation at a glance and surrendered without any delay, and were once more placed in irons.[15]

Shortly after the failed escape attempt, McCall offered to turn state's evidence and said he had been paid by John Varnes of Deadwood to murder Hickok. According to McCall, as reported in the *Black Hills Pioneer*: "It appears that some time ago Wild Bill and Varnes had a difficulty in Denver and the animosity between the two was augmented by a dispute over a game of poker at the 'Senate' saloon in [Deadwood], at which time Bill interfered in a dispute between Varnes and another man. Bill covered Varnes with his pistol and arrogated to himself the position of umpire, after which his friends interfered and ended the difficulty."[16]

Federal officials did not believe McCall's story, however, and the newspaper printed a notice from Deputy U.S. Marshal H. C. Ash the following week:

November 12, 1876.

I, the undersigned, do declare that the statement published in the PIONEER of the 11th inst. is a fabrication cut from the whole cloth as no warrant has been issued for John Varnes.[17]

Lorenzo Hickok arrived in Yankton on November 27 for the beginning of the trial, which was postponed until December 1 for the arrival of more witnesses. When court reconvened, Marshal J. H. Burdick informed the court that none of McCall's witnesses could be found, so defense counsel Oliver Shannon asked presiding judge P. C. Shannon (any relation is not clear) for a continuance until April. When the judge denied the request the following day, McCall "used some language which wasn't very complimentary to the court...."[18]

At ten o'clock on the morning of December 4, the United States vs. John McCall, alias Jack McCall, began. Selected for the jury were John Treadway, H. A. Dunham, William Box,

George Pike, Lewis Clark, West Negus, Charles Edwards, I. N. Esmay, H. T. Mowery, Nelson Armstrong, J. A. Withie, and M. L. Winchell. Treadway was chosen foreman and Edwards secretary. After the jury was sworn in, court adjourned until two o'clock that afternoon. At that time U.S. Attorney William Pound called his first witness, George M. Shingle, who had been living in Cheyenne for the past nine months.

As in the case of most civilian trials of the period, transcripts have not survived — if any were ever recorded. A few motions and affidavits are in the National Archives branch in Kansas City, Missouri, but most of the testimony, although not the questions, was printed in the *Yankton Press and Dakotaian*. Shingle told the court that he had been in the saloon weighing gold dust when the defendant entered, came up behind Hickok, put a pistol two or three feet behind the gunman's head, and fired. "The table where Wild Bill sat was nearly in the middle of the room," Shingle said. "He was facing the bar."[19]

McCall's attorneys then requested that prosecution witnesses not be present in the courtroom while other witnesses for the prosecution were on the stand. Judge Shannon agreed, and, after the removal of witnesses, Shingle continued his testimony.

During the miner's court trial, Shingle testified, McCall said "that he had killed Wild Bill and that he was glad of it, and if he had to do it over he would do the same thing — that Bill had killed a brother of his and he did it for revenge."[20]

During the cross-examination of Shingle, Oliver Shannon or General W. H. H. Beadle apparently tried to bring Hickok's fondness for drink into play. Shingle said Hickok was "a constant drinker" but was "sober when the shooting occurred."[21]

Shingle said he could not tell if McCall had been drunk when he shot Hickok.

Next called to the stand was Carl Mann, who also described the shooting of Hickok as well as the previous meeting between the deceased and the defendant.

> Bill was there and McCall weighed out some gold dust to get some chips to play poker with Bill and others. McCall won $23 or $24. Am not certain of the amount. He then went outdoors and came back and played again and bet five or six dollars and Bill bet twenty or twenty-five more. McCall shoved his purse further onto the table and says "I call you." Bill won and they came to the bar and asked me to weigh out $20 or $25. The purse was $16.25 short. Bill said "you owe me $16.25." McCall said "yes," and went out. He came back shortly and Bill said "did I break you?" McCall said "yes." Bill gave him all the change he had, 75 cents, to buy his supper with and told him that if he quit winner in the game he was playing he would give him more. McCall would not take the money and went out in fifteen or twenty minutes."[22]

One discrepancy the defense team did not attack was the murder weapon. Shingle testified that McCall used "a Sharps improved revolver 18 inches long with a piece of buckskin sewed around the stock." Mann called it "a navy size revolver." The weapon McCall used remains a mystery.

After Mann was cross-examined, court recessed until nine o'clock the next day, when Captain William Massie testified.

Massie's account of the Hickok murder followed along the same lines as Shingle's and Mann's, but he also said he saw McCall enter the saloon a day or two earlier and might have been about to try to kill Hickok then. "I saw the defendant...walk around behind Bill and pull his pistol about two thirds out," Massie said. "There was a young man with him who put his arm around the defendant and walked him towards the back door."[23]

Joseph Mitchell, now living in Sioux City, also described the murder, and again the cross-examination, if there was one, did nothing to aid McCall's case. U.S. Attorney William Pound then called General William P. Dewey, H. H. Reed, and Ed F. Higbee to testify as to the location of Deadwood and prove that the city was in Dakota Territory and thus within the court's jurisdiction. The final prosecution witness was jailer J. B. Robinson, who detailed the escape attempt of McCall and McCarty.

The prosecution rested at five o'clock that afternoon, at which time the defense counsels informed Judge Shannon that they had no witnesses. Instead, the attorneys filed a motion that McCall be discharged because the prosecutor had never served a true copy of the indictment.

The defense also objected on the grounds that the case was outside the court's jurisdiction and requested a new trial. On December 6 Judge Shannon ruled against the defense.

Pound made his closing argument that afternoon, followed by Oliver Shannon and Beadle — what they said has not been recorded — and at seven o'clock, Judge Shannon charged the jury. The twelve men deliberated until almost midnight, at which time they returned to the courtroom. Foreman John Treadway read the written verdict: "We the jurors in the case of the United States vs. John McCall, alias Jack McCall find a verdict of guilty of murder as charged in the indictment."[24]

The *Dakota Herald* reported: "The defendant had no witnesses to testify in his behalf, but the evidence against him was full and clear, and his conviction of murder was rendered in an easy matter. The penalty in this case is death by hanging, but Judge Shannon has not yet passed sentence upon the doomed man."[25]

After the verdict, Jack McCall waited in his cell, reading a Bible, and visited with a Catholic priest on December 12, while Shannon and Beadle prepared a motion for a new trial, which was filed on December 16. The main points the defense brought up were: "1st, no jurisdiction of the court; 2nd, that a correct copy of the indictment had not been served upon the defendant; 3rd, and that the jury during the trial visited saloons and drank there and that they had liquors in their room at night."[26] Judge Shannon again denied the defense motion, and a sentencing date was set for January 31, 1877, which was later moved up to January 3. On that day, Judge Shannon ruled that McCall:

> ...be remanded hence to the place whence you came, that you be then imprisoned until Thursday, the first day of March, A.D. 1877, upon which day you shall thence be conducted to the place of execution, where, between the hours of nine o'clock in the forenoon and two o'clock in the afternoon of the said day, you shall be hanged by the neck until you shall be dead.
>
> And may the Lord have mercy upon your soul.[27]

McCall's attorney filed a writ of error with the Supreme Court of Dakota Territory, arguing again that McCall had not been served properly and that the federal court had no jurisdiction over the case. On January 19, 1877, the court rejected the appeal:

> By having entered upon trial, and by having waited until the prosecution closed its case, the defendant was too late to make the objections referred to, concerning those copies; for, by such conduct and acquiescence, he virtually admitted that he had a copy sufficient for all purposes intended by the act of Congress.
>
> As to the objection that the defendant should have been indicted and tried on the other side of this court, it is well settled that a trial for homicide, committed in an Indian reserve, must be had on the Federal side of a Territorial court....[28]

All the justices concurred. Shannon and Beadle tried to get the sentence commuted to life in prison, and Governor John L. Pennington signed the petition and forwarded it to President Ulysses S. Grant. The petition was denied, and Marshal Burdick received the death warrant on February 14. He announced that the execution would be private. "Numerous requests have been presented him asking for a public execution of the hanging of McCall," the *Press and Dakotaian* reported, "but he rightly decides against thus gratifying morbid curiosity."[29]

In the end, however, an estimated one thousand people would attend the "private" execution.

Aftermath

The gallows were to be constructed near the federal jail, but neighborhood residents objected, so the scaffold was put up two miles north of Yankton in the school section of the Catholic cemetery. McCall seemed resigned to his fate, reading the Bible and visiting frequently with Roman Catholic priest Father John Daxacher. He politely refused visitations from two local ministers, the Reverend Jos. Ward of the Congregational church and the Reverend J. A. Motter of the M.E. church. McCall "appeared to recall his sentence as just," the *Black Hills Pioneer* reported, "and evidently endeavored to go prepared to enter the next world in a proper spirit."[30]

While the press waited for him to make some comment, he fired off a note to the *Press and Dakotaian* on February 21.

> Sirs: — I intend to write an article which I wish you to publish in your paper after my death. If you will be here the day the execution takes place, I will hand it to you. If you accept or decline to publish it, please let me know.
>
> John McCall[31]

Whatever McCall intended to say — whether explaining his motive for murdering Hickok, implicating Varnes, etc. — was lost forever when he burned the papers the night before his execution. According to some sources, McCall received a letter from his sister, who lived in Louisville, Kentucky, the night before his execution, and the condemned man spent the rest of the night composing a reply. James Noonan, a deputy U.S. marshal in charge of the jail at the time, later recalled McCall's last night:

On the night before he was to be hung, a letter arrived from [McCall's] mother and sister, who lived in Tennessee. He cried as he read the letter over and over. Finally he asked for a pencil and he scratched off a reply and sealed the envelope. He said he had just written to his mother that he had only ten hours to live.[32]

Likewise, the letter to his mother (or sister), if Noonan's memory was correct, has been lost to history.

On a dreary, wet Thursday morning, March 1, 1877, John "Jack" McCall was escorted to the gallows. It would be the first legal hanging in Dakota Territory, as the headline in the *Dakota Herald* proclaimed "THE HANGMAN'S ROPE. It Is Legitimately Stretched in Yankton for the First Time."[33]

The *Press and Dakotaian* reported:

This morning dawned cloudily, with a drizzling rain, the heavens seemingly draped in somber colorings for some specially dreadful occasion. At half past eight o'clock we were admitted to the United States jail, where we found U.S. Marshal Burdick, Deputy Marshals C. P. Edmunds and Stanley, Rev. Father Daxacher, and J. A. Curry, his assistant. The Rev. Father was then engaged in religious ministrations with the condemned man, who seemed resigned to his fate. His fellow prisoners, McCarty and Allen, seemed more moved by the solemn ceremonies than McCall.[34]

Marshal Burdick read the death warrant at nine o'clock, and McCall's irons were removed. He and Daxacher talked quietly, and McCall's cellmates hung their heads in silence. At nine-thirty McCall, dressed in plain black broadcloth suit and collarless white shirt, said goodbye to Allen and McCarty and left the federal jail, accompanied by Daxacher, Curry, Burdick, deputies Edmunds, Ash, and Stanley, and special guard George D. Mathieson. Also with the group were reporters from the *Dakota Herald, Yankton Press and Dakotaian, New York Herald*, and a New England journal. Burdick and Ash climbed into a small carriage and led the way to the execution site, followed by another carriage carrying McCall and the others. "McCall continued to bear up bravely, even after the gallows loomed in full view."[35]

The gallows consisted of four upright posts, 6x6 inches, 8 feet 10 inches apart on the ground, 15 feet 4 inches high, on the top of which were plates which supported a cross-beam in the center, the whole being well braced. It was closely boarded up to the drop, which was 7 feet 10 inches from the ground, the lower part thus presenting the appearance of a huge dry-goods box, with a door facing the east. The floor was provided with a trap-door, the mechanical contrivance for the swinging of which we did not learn. A one-inch cotton rope, with the fatal noose, was attached to the cross-beam. On the western side of the structure were steps leading up to the floor, by means of which an ascent could be made without being subject to the scrutiny of the crowd, who were stationed on the eastern side. It certainly was not altogether attractive, even if a novelty in Dakota. There is said to be an eternal order of fitness in every thing, and the erection of a gallows in such close proximity to the graveyard is a striking illustration of this fact.[36]

At ten o'clock McCall reached the execution site. Deputy Marshal Ash, wearing white gloves, took McCall's left arm and escorted him up the gallows. McCall "placed himself in the center of the platform facing east and gazed out over the throng without exhibiting the least faltering; not even a quiver of the lip."[37] In addition to McCall and Ash, Burdick, Daxacher, and Curry stood on the scaffold.

After his limbs were pinioned, McCall knelt with "his spiritual counsel" in prayer. When he rose, he kissed the crucifix. Marshal Burdick placed a black cap and noose around McCall's head. "Wait one moment, Marshal, until I pray," McCall said, and Burdick obliged. When McCall finished praying, Burdick adjusted the noose. "Draw it tighter, Marshal," McCall said.

All was now in readiness, and the assemblance of nearly one thousand persons seemed to hold their breath. It was an awful moment — the single step between life and death. At precisely fifteen minutes after ten o'clock the trap was sprung, and with the single choking expression "Oh God," uttered while the drop fell the body of John McCall was dangling between heaven and earth. The drop was four feet and everything having been carefully arranged there was but a brief struggle with the King of Terrors."[38]

Twelve minutes later Doctors D. F. Etter and J. M. Miller examined McCall. The drop had failed to break the condemned man's neck. McCall was still alive, and still holding the crucifix. He dangled strangling for ten more minutes before death was pronounced. Afterward his body was placed in a walnut coffin and buried in the cemetery.

Under the headline "Another Ruffian Gone," L. D. F. Poore's report of the execution appeared in the March 2 edition of the *New York Herald.*

Jack McCall, the murderer of "Wild Bill," left the world yesterday at Yankton, Neb., [sic] in a manner quite unusual to the border ruffian, but none the less effectual on that account. It is not often that a man of his style kills another without establishing some claim for gratitude upon respectable society; but McCall's victim was a man who, in spite of many faults, had done much good and needed service to society and his country, while the murderer never served either, except when he shuffled off his own mortal coil. The best that can be said of him is that, although he lived like a ruffian, he died like a man. Trying to maintain his stolidity, he nevertheless spent his last moments with the crucifix clasped tightly in his hands as he engaged in silent prayer, and as the drop fell there escaped from his lips the holy name which his associates had never before heard him utter with due respect. The world is better off by having lost him. Men of his type are worse than useless, and the most tender humanitarians despair of ever changing their natures. His fate may terrify into comparative quiet such creatures of his kind as have hitherto trusted that they were to be a law unto themselves; and thus Jack McCall in dying may have served the world to which while living he was an unqualified curse.[39]

A historical marker in Yankton commemorates the hanging of Jack McCall, but "McCall's grave is still a well-kept secret in Yankton, and like losing the state capital, folks in Yankton would just rather not remember it."[40] Compare that to the bustling gambling/tourist town of Deadwood, South Dakota, where Wild Bill Hickok is murdered over and over again each summer, and the miner's court trial of Jack McCall is re-created for tourists — and has been for several years. Hickok's grave — he was reburied in the Mount Moriah cemetery on August 3, 1879 — is also a popular tourist destination. Frontier heroine Calamity Jane, at her insistence, is buried beside him.

Most of the principals in the Yankton trial faded into obscurity. Judge Granville Bennett, whose Dakota Supreme Court ruling paved the way for McCall's execution, would move to Deadwood in 1877 and oversee the city's first legal judicial court. His daughter, Estelline Bennett, would go on to write a popular and highly readable memoir of the raucous frontier town, *Old Deadwood Days*, first published in 1928.

But the man most responsible for bringing Jack McCall to justice did not live to see it carried out.

Colonel George May arrived in Yankton in October to help with McCall's prosecution. "When he arrived in Yankton," the *Dakota Herald* noted, "he was without any means, or in common parlance, was financially 'broke.' He was promised a portion of the fee money from his client but was unable to get it. He soon became acquainted with the members of the bar of this city. A subscription paper was passed around, which gave him sufficient funds to relieve him of his pressing embarrassment."[41]

May came down with an undisclosed illness, however, and died at the Merchants Hotel on November 21, a week before the McCall trial was scheduled to begin. A funeral was held at the Episcopal church on November 22, and May was buried in the city cemetery.

After leaving the Black Hills, John Varnes was rumored to have met his end violently in Colorado or Arizona. Whether he was actually involved in Hickok's death will probably never be known.

The bullet that killed Hickok remained lodged in Captain William Massie's arm for several years. The old ham would often greet strangers and friends with a "Shake the hand with the ball that killed Wild Bill." He continued to do this, the legend goes, even after he had the ball removed. Massie died in 1910.

More than four years after his death, Jack McCall would be in the Dakota Territory news once again. In 1881 the bodies interred in the Yankton Catholic cemetery were dug up to be reburied in a new graveyard. Upon opening McCall's coffin, "It was discovered that McCall had been buried with the rope around his neck that strangled him."[42]

Chapter Notes

Primary sources: *Frontier Days: A True Narrative of Striking Events on the Western Frontier* (J. M. and H. L. Kuykendall, 1917) by W. L. Kuykendall; *The West of Wild Bill Hickok* (University of Oklahoma Press, 1982), *They Called Him Wild Bill* (University of Oklahoma Press, 1974) and *Alias Jack McCall* (Kansas Posse of the Westerners, 1967), all by Joseph G. Rosa; *Pioneer Days in the Black Hills by One of the Early Day Pioneers* (University of Oklahoma Press, 2000) by John S. McClintock; *Wild Bill Hickok: Deadwood City End of Trail* (Old West Alive! Publishing, 2001) by Thadd Turner; The United States versus John McCall, alias Jack McCall. Trial documents, 1876-1877, Federal Records Center, National Archives-Central Plains Region; and various 1876-77 editions of the *Black Hills Daily Pioneer,* the *Dakota Herald,* and the *Yankton Press and Dakotaian.*

1. "A Trip to the Black Hills," *Scribner's Monthly*, April 1877, p. 755.

2. Rosa, Joseph G. *They Called Him Wild Bill*, pp. 292-293.

3. McClintock, John C., *Pioneer Days in the Black Hills: Acurate History and Facts Related by One of the Early Day Pioneers*, published by the University of Oklahoma Press, 2000, p. 107. Reprinted by Permission. All rights reserved.

4. Turner, Thadd, *Wild Bill Hickok: Deadwood City — End of Trail*, p. 80.

5. *Yankton Press and Dakotaian*, December 5, 1876.

6. *Sioux City Journal* clipping, no date, McCall File, South Dakota State Archives.

7. Defined by Ramon F. Adams in *Western Words: A Dictionary of the American West* as "an independent court of justice set up by miners remote from settled regions."

8. *Scribner's Monthly*, April 1877, p. 755.

9. Kuykendall, W. L., *Frontier Days*, p. 188. The judge's memory is faulty as to the number of people in the No. 10 at the time of Hickok's murder.

10. *Black Hills Pioneer*, August 5, 1876.

11. Kuykendall, p. 189. Some reports say McCall fled Deadwood immediately. Others say he waited a few days before taking flight. An immediate departure would seemingly have been more prudent.

12. Ibid.

13. *Dakota Herald*, September 9, 1876.

14. Printed in the *Black Hills Pioneer*, September 9, 1876.

15. *Yankton Press and Dakotaian*, November 10, 1876.

16. *Black Hills Pioneer*, November 11, 1876.

17. *Black Hills Pioneer*, November 18, 1876.

18. *Yankton Press and Dakotaian*, December 3, 1876.

19. *Yankton Press and Dakotaian*, December 5, 1876.

20. Ibid.

21. Ibid.

22. Ibid.

23. *Yankton Press and Dakotaian*, December 6, 1876.

24. The United States versus John McCall, alias Jack McCall. Trial documents, 1876-1877.

25. *Dakota Herald*, December 9, 1876.

26. *Yankton Press and Dakotaian*, December 17, 1876.

27. *Dakota Herald*, January 6, 1877.

28. Bennett, Granville G., *Reports of Cases Argued and Determined in the Supreme Court of the Territory of Dakota, from its Organization to and including the December Term*, 1877, p. 334.

29. *Yankton Press and Dakotaian*, February 15, 1877.

30. *Black Hills Pioneer*, March 10, 1877.

31. *Yankton Press and Dakotaian*, February 28, 1877.

32. *Sioux City Journal* clipping, no date. McCall file. South Dakota State Archives.

33. *Dakota Herald*, March 6, 1877.

34. *Yankton Press and Dakotaian*, March 1, 1877.

35. Ibid.

36. *Dakota Herald*, March 6, 1877.

37. *Yankton Press and Dakotaian*, March 1, 1877.

38. *Yankton Press and Dakotaian*, March 1, 1877.

39. *New York Herald*, March 2, 1877.

40. *Black Hills Weekly*, February 26, 1976.

41. *Dakota Herald*, November 25, 1876.

42. *Black Hills Daily Times*, June 30, 1881.

"I am that d——d desperado, John Wesley Hardin"

Trial of John Wesley Hardin

«⟵————————————⟶»

Comanche, Texas, 1877

Prelude

He has been called the greatest gunfighter who ever lived, and one of the most ruthless. After all, this is the Texas-born shootist, those legends say, who killed a man sleeping in a Kansas hotel because he was snoring too loudly. John Wesley Hardin is said to have killed twenty to fifty men. Author Eugene Cunningham credits him with forty kills, but other historians pare that number down to around twenty, although no matter the number, Hardin lived a violent life in a relatively short period. He shot his first man when he was fifteen years old in 1868 and was sent to prison ten years later for one of his many killings.

Wyatt Earp, Billy the Kid, and Wild Bill Hickok might have more name recognition, but many writers believe Wes Hardin was the best gunman ever to strap on a holster. He even might have caused Hickok to back down during a confrontation in Abilene, Kansas, in 1871. Or maybe that's just a myth as well.

Texas is full of John Wesley Hardin stories. Consider this one told by Thalias Newton McKinney of Uvalde: "One time, John Wesley Hardin stayed camped on my father's ranch about ten days. I used to take him butter and eggs and he would pay me for them. He used to pay me to put a white piece of paper or board on a tree and cut a small black spot in the center of the paper. He could hit it with a pistol 75 yards and 200 yards with a Winchester. He was the best shot I ever saw."[1]

True story or Texas bull? It doesn't matter. No one disputes Hardin's accuracy with a firearm.

The second son of circuit-riding Methodist minister James G. and Elizabeth Hardin, Wes Hardin entered a rapidly changing Texas frontier on May 26, 1853, at Blair's Springs on Bois d'Arc Creek near Bonham. When the Civil War broke out, the nine-year-old boy wanted to enlist in the Confederate army with a cousin to fight the Yankees, but his father ended that dream with a corporal beating. The war would have a lasting effect on Hardin and might explain his foray into bloodshed as a teen-ager and adult. In his autobiography, published in 1896, a year after his death, Hardin explained:

> I had seen Abraham Lincoln burned and shot to pieces in effigy so often that I looked upon him as a very demon incarnate, who was waging a relentless and cruel war on the South to rob her of her most sacred rights. So you can see that the justice of the Southern cause was taught to me in my youth, and if I never relinquished these teachings in after years, surely I was but true to my early training. The way you bend a twig, that is the way it will grow, is an old saying, and a true one. So I grew up a rebel.[2]

In 1861 Hardin witnessed a senseless brawl that left one man dead. A few years later Hardin had become violent himself. In 1867 Hardin and schoolmate Charles Sloter got in a row over

Texas gunman John Wesley Hardin as a young man.
(Western History Collections, University of Oklahoma Library)

graffiti written on the wall about a girl at the school. Hardin
stabbed Sloter in the chest and back and almost killed him,
but instead of being expelled (according to Hardin anyway)

the school trustees exonerated him for his actions, and Sloter (again according to Hardin) was lynched many years later.

Violence continued. A year after the schoolyard incident, the fifteen-year-old Hardin got into an argument with a powerfully built former slave named Mage in Polk County. After a wrestling match involving Mage, Hardin, and Hardin's cousin, Barnett Jones, got out of hand, the ex-slave threatened to kill Hardin but was thrown off the property. The next day Hardin met Mage on the road. They argued again, and, Hardin said, when the big man came at him with a stick, threatening to kill the teen, he shot him repeatedly with his .44-caliber Colt revolver. Hardin left the mortally wounded man and returned with an uncle and another man and explained what had happened. "Mage still showed fight and called me a liar," Hardin recalled. "If it had not been for my uncle, I would have shot him again."[3]

When Mage died that November, Hardin's parents were distraught. Under the postwar Reconstruction government, Texas was quickly becoming factional. On one side were white Unionists, Radical Republicans, and the new freedmen, including a powerful state police comprising black and white officers. On the other side were Southern-sympathizing Democrats and hotheaded bigots. John Wesley Hardin would soon become the working-class hero/killer of the racists and anti-Unionists and a demon for Governor Edmund Davis and the law. Believing that Hardin would surely be hanged for killing a black man under the current political regime, Hardin's parents persuaded him to flee.

Hardin took off to his older brother's place north of Sumpter, Texas, where he said he killed three soldiers looking for him. His friends and neighbors took the dead men's horses and burned their belongings to keep the killings hush-hush.

By January Hardin was in Navarro County, teaching school, but that fall he had moved on. He worked, he gambled, he cowboyed, he killed. Or so he said. Hardin's autobiography often provides the only, and frequently uncorroborated, clues to his early life as a fugitive. Consider this often-repeated story of his confrontation with Abilene marshal Wild Bill Hickok:

> Wild Bill whirled around and met me. He said, "What are you howling about, and what are you doing with those pistols on?"
>
> I said, "I am just taking in the town."
>
> He pulled his pistol and said, "Take those pistols off. I arrest you."
>
> I said all right and pulled them out of the scabbard, but while he was reaching for them, I reversed them and whirled them over on him with the muzzles in his face, springing back at the same time. I told him to put his pistols up, which he did. I cursed him for a long-haired scoundrel that would shoot a boy with his back to him (as I had been told he intended to do me). He said, "Little Arkansaw, you have been wrongly informed."
>
> I shouted, "This is my fight and I'll kill the first man that fires a gun."
>
> Bill said, "You are the gamest and quickest boy I ever saw. Let us compromise this matter and I will be your friend. Let us go in here and take a drink, as I want to talk to you and give you some advice."
>
> At first I thought he might be trying to get the drop on me, but he finally convinced me of his good intentions, and we went in and took a drink. We went into a

private room and I had a long talk with him and we came out friends.[4]

Historians have debated the confrontation since Hardin's 1896 autobiography, which is the only account of the showdown. By the time it was published, John Wesley Hardin had been planted in El Paso's Concordia Cemetery for a year and James Butler "Wild Bill" Hickok had been buried in Deadwood, South Dakota, for twenty years.

Joseph G. Rosa, the preeminent biographer of Wild Bill, says the story is likely nothing more than Hardin's delusions of grandeur. El Pasoan Leon C. Metz, who won a Spur Award from Western Writers of America for his outstanding 1996 biography of Hardin, says there is no reason to doubt the story's veracity. No surprise there, but as much as I respect both historians, I'll have to side with Rosa on this one.

Regardless of what happened in Kansas, Hardin was no one to trifle with. He returned to Texas and killing but made time to marry fourteen-year-old Jane Bowen on February 29, 1872. They made their home in Gonzales County, although Hardin was soon on the road again. Recovering from buckshot wounds sustained during another gunfight, Hardin surrendered to Cherokee County Sheriff Dick Reagan, a fifty-one-year-old Tennessee native whom the gunman respected, in early September 1872 and was taken to Austin later that month. With murder indictments awaiting him back in Gonzales, Hardin was on the road again, escorted by four state policemen. The prisoner and lawmen arrived safely, and Hardin's shackles were removed. Interim sheriff William E. Jones took charge of the prisoner and allegedly told him not to worry, that Hardin had friends in this neck of the woods.

That he did. Slipped a saw, Hardin cut through the iron bars that fall and made his escape. He returned to "darling and beloved wife" Jane, dabbling in the cattle business, but soon was involved in the 1873-74 Sutton-Taylor feud in Central Texas.

The Sutton-Taylor confrontation was a product of turbulent postwar Texas. Virginia-born Josiah Taylor had settled in DeWitt County, and his family, including sons Creed and Pitkin, kin, and friends bled Confederate blood. On the other side stood the Suttons, led by patriarch William E. Sutton, a Fayette County native who had moved to DeWitt County. The Suttons were backed by the Texas State Police, founded on July 1, 1870, and Reconstruction government. Considering the mood and climate, the violence that broke out was not surprising.

Both families were a violent breed. When a black sergeant showed up at a dance in 1866, Buck Taylor killed him. That same year another black soldier was shot and killed by Hays Taylor at some Indianola saloon. In November of the following year, Hays and brother Doby killed two Union soldiers in Mason. The next spring Deputy Sheriff William Sutton and a posse caught up with a gang of horse thieves in Bastrop, where they killed Charley Taylor and captured James Sharp, who was then conveniently killed during an alleged escape attempt on the way to Clinton.

On Christmas Eve 1868 Buck Taylor and Dick Chisholm were killed in Clinton in a gunfight after questioning William Sutton's honesty. Sutton was soon backed by the Texas State Police and Captain Jack Helm, along with Jim Cox and Joe Tumlinson, and the police force soon clashed with Southern sympathizers — especially the Taylors. Hays Taylor was killed by ambush on August 23, 1869. One year later a posse arrested Pitkin Taylor's sons-in-law, Henry and William Kelly, and murdered the two a few miles from their home. Henry's wife witnessed the cold-blooded killings, and Helm was soon booted off the police force although he managed to keep his job as DeWitt County sheriff.

After Pitkin Taylor, an old man by then, was shot down in his cornfield — after being lured outside by a cow bell — and died six months later in 1872, his son, Jim, swore revenge. William Sutton was ambushed and wounded in April and June of 1873, but escaped. Jim Cox, ambushed later that summer, wasn't as lucky; he and another Sutton supporter were killed.

Into this cauldron rode John Wesley Hardin. Violent and racist by nature — despite what Hardin apologists may say — Hardin sided with the Taylors.

Hardin and Jim Taylor arrived in Albuquerque, Texas, in western Gonzales County sometime between May and June 1873. Hardin said he came to the town to meet with Sheriff Jack Helm for some unrecorded purpose — perhaps to kill him.

Helm remains a bit of a mystery. He might have cowboyed for Abel "Shanghai" Pierce shortly after the Civil War before being appointed special assistant under Captain C. S. Bell to bring order to Bee, San Patricio, Wilson, DeWitt, and Goliad Counties. Helm and his regulators reportedly killed twenty-one men in two months during the summer of 1869 while capturing only ten men alive. He was appointed one of four captains in the Texas State Police in 1870 and continued his bloody reign of terror. That got him kicked off the police force, which itself was disbanded in April 1873, and he settled down in Albuquerque to work on his invention, a cotton-worm destroyer.

Hardin had taken his horse to the town blacksmith's shop when he heard Helm call out: "Hands up, you son of a bitch!" Hardin turned to see the lawman approaching Taylor with a large knife. "Someone hollered, 'Shoot the d——d scoundrel.' It appeared to me that Helms was the scoundrel, so I grabbed my shotgun and fired at Capt. Jack Helms as he was closing with Jim Taylor."[5]

Hardin pointed his gun at the townsmen while Taylor shot Helm several times in the head. Hardin said Helm "fell with twelve buckshot in his breast and several six-shooter balls in his head. All of this happened in the midst of his own friends and advisors, who stood by utterly amazed. The news soon spread that I had killed Jack Helms and I received many letters of thanks from the widows of men whom he had cruelly

The Killing of Jack Helms, as illustrated in Hardin's posthumously published autobiography. (*The Life of John Wesley Hardin*, copyright 1896)

put to death. Many of the best citizens of Gonzales and DeWitt counties patted me on the back and told me that was the best act of my life."[6]

A truce briefly stopped the Sutton-Taylor war, but violence returned in December when Taylor-backer Wiley Pridgen was murdered in Thomaston. Sutton eventually moved to Victoria but was shot down, along with a friend, by Jim and Bill Taylor while boarding a steamer at the port city of Indianola on March 11, 1874. Three Taylors were then lynched in retaliation. Meanwhile, Hardin was back in the cattle business — more likely cattle rustling — and had sent a herd north. Three of his cowboys were arrested in Hamilton, charged with rustling, and returned to Clinton, where they were lynched on June 20, 1874.

Soon the newly formed Texas Rangers tried to bring peace to Central Texas, but they had little luck. Bill Taylor was arrested and tried for murder, but he escaped during the great Indianola hurricane of September 15, 1875. Jim Taylor met his end on December 27 in Clinton after he and friends murdered Sutton leader Rube Brown, Cuero's marshal, and was then gunned down in the streets. With all the principals dead or in hiding, the Sutton-Taylor feud had bled itself out.

Hardin's brother Joe had married and settled down in Comanche County, Texas, where he practiced law, became a Mason and county treasurer, and invited his parents and family to move up there with him. Hardin's wife, Jane, and daughter, Mollie, went to Comanche first, and by January 1874 the gunman had joined them.

The town of Comanche, in the county's center, had been established in 1858 and became county seat the next year, replacing Cora, although the town wasn't incorporated until 1873. The post office came in 1860, and a newspaper, the

Chief, set up operations in 1873. Located a hundred miles southwest of Fort Worth, Comanche was soon supplying ranchers.

Hardin gambled and managed his cattle affairs — even registering a brand despite accusations of rustling — raced horses, and drank while brother Joe managed a few shady land practices, none of which made the Hardins popular in Comanche.

Joe Hardin, brother of the infamous gunman, was misidentified as John Wesley Hardin in the gunfighter's autobiography.
(The Life of John Wesley Hardin, copyright 1896)

During a town festival on May 26, 1874, Hardin won some horse races and drank heavily. He carried a hideout gun, although the town prohibited the carrying of weapons. Hardin must have been pretty well roostered when Deputy Sheriff Charles Webb, armed with two revolvers, approached him around sundown.

"Here comes that damned Brown County sheriff," cohort Dave Carnes said. Five paces from Hardin, Webb stopped, and Hardin asked menacingly: "Have you any papers for my arrest?"[7]

"I don't know you," Webb replied.

"My name is John Wesley Hardin."

"Now I know you but have no papers for your arrest."

Webb had his hands behind his back while Hardin maintained a belligerent tone and eventually asked what Webb held in his hands. The deputy showed him a cigar, and Hardin relaxed and invited Webb into the nearest saloon for a drink and a smoke. Webb agreed.

Hardin said when he turned, Webb pulled a pistol. Hardin's friend, Bud Dixon, shouted a warning, and Hardin spun around and drew his own weapon. Webb shot first, the bullet cutting a gash across Hardin's side, a painful wound, but Hardin kept his composure and sent a slug into Webb's left cheek. Webb slammed against a wall, fired a round into the air, while Dixon and Jim Taylor riddled Webb's body with bullets. Another man, Frank Wilson, then tried to draw his gun, but Hardin covered him with his pistol.

The account in his autobiography was written many years after the killing. In 1877, with the shootout fresher in his mind, Hardin told reporters:

> I had no acquaintance with Charles Webb. I was in the back portion of a bar-room — at the back door —

Jack Wright's bar-room. Had been civil and had no difficulty with any one in Comanche county up to this
time. Webb was talking to a party to the right of the
back door. I was on the left talking to another. While
standing thus I was told Webb was the deputy sheriff
of Brown county. I asked to be introduced to him. After
finishing his talk with the party he started to pass me,
when I spoke to him. As he turned on me he pulled his
pistol and commenced firing on me. When he pulled
his pistol I started to argue with him upon the question of the difference between us. He did not hesitate,
but fired, when I jumped to one side. The bullet
passed through my clothes on the left side, grazing the
skin. Bud Dixon and Jim Taylor, my friends, being
present, and seeing that Webb had the drop on me,
commenced to defend me with their pistols. Webb got
his second shot when he was down upon his knees.
The boys still fired, and during all this time I fired not
one single time, seeing that Webb was already equally
matched. If the boys had not fired upon Webb, I, of
course, would have fired as soon as possible. Webb
fired the third shot after he got on his knees. He died
immediately afterwards.[8]

Of course, when Hardin made that statement, he was in custody and soon to stand trial for Webb's murder. Was he telling
the truth? Partly so, perhaps, although he likely had a hand in
shooting Webb. Hardin continued:

The sheriff of Comanche county came at this time
upon the scene, when I handed him my pistol and said
to him, "I claim your protection." At the same time
another squad came up firing, headed by Henry Ware,

John Wesley Hardin's autobiography was published in 1896 after his death in Seguin, Texas, and remains in print today. (Author's Collection)

a Comanche outlaw and one of Webb's friends. I broke and ran to the first horse and so did Taylor. They kept firing on us. We got on the horses and made our escape. Dixon went too, but was arrested two days afterwards.

The same day that Dixon was arrested my father, mother and wife were arrested by Waller's Rangers and placed under guard. My younger brother and Dixon, neither of whom had anything to do with the affair, were also arrested. The Dixons are my cousins. These two boys, J. G. Hardin and Tom Dixon, aged respectively 23 and 17, were hung by a mob, and the other Dixon was taken out of jail and hung too. The hanging occurred at Comanche. My brother Joe was a Mason, and belonged to the Comanche lodge and was in good standing. They made every effort to take me, saying they would give me no law but the rope.[9]

In his autobiography, Hardin said he later learned Webb had planned to assassinate him. He claimed self-defense, although the *Dallas Weekly Herald* called it murder and said the killers were members of a gang of cattle thieves. Charles Webb was buried as a Mason in Brownwood's Greenleaf Cemetery.

Fifty-seven-year-old Texas Ranger Captain John R. Waller arrived in Comanche with fifty-five men on May 27 and began scouring the countryside for John Wesley Hardin. Hardin and Jim Taylor clashed with five rangers three days later but escaped. As Hardin mentioned, Joe Hardin and the Dixon brothers, Bud and Tom, were captured and lynched. John Wesley Hardin rode south. On January 25, 1875, a joint resolution of the Texas State Legislature put a price on the killer's head: $4,000. Hardin fled east, to Alabama and later Florida, while Texas authorities kept a close eye on Hardin's friends and family.

After intercepting a letter addressed to a J. H. Swain of Pollard, Alabama, Jack Duncan, who had been working undercover for the rangers, and Lieutenant John B. Armstrong took off to bring in the fugitive. In Pollard, Duncan learned that Hardin, alias Swain, had gone to Pensacola, Florida, to do a little gambling. Working with Florida law enforcement and Pensacola Railroad general manager W. D. Chipley, the two rangers waited to spring their trap on a railroad car, believing that would be the best spot — and least dangerous — to arrest Hardin.

On August 23, 1877, Hardin and several chums boarded the smoking car. The law moved in.

Detective Duncan, who knew Hardin, took his position on the opposite side of the car from the depot building to prevent his escape; Lieutenant Armstrong and Mr. Chipley entered the front of the car, while the sheriff and his deputy at the same time entered the rear of the car. Hardin and a companion named Mann were sitting together in a seat at the rear end of the car, and the moment Lieutenant Armstrong, who held in his hand a large pistol, stepped upon the front platform, Hardin saw the pistol, and he afterwards stated that he instantly suspected that there was something up which "smelt of Texas business," and he also said, had he not at that moment been seized by two men who entered just behind him he would have fired on Lieutenant Armstrong; but fate was at last against him, and now it was himself that was to be roughly handled. The moment he was seized, Mann arose and fired three fortunately harmless shots, when several shots were fired at him. Mann then jumped out of a car window and started to run, but was again fired upon and killed. Hardin was, in the meantime, struggling fearfully against great odds, but with four men hold of him the contest could not last long or result seriously. He did all that a brave and desperate man could do to gain his liberty, and when a pistol was pointed at his head he said, "shoot and be damned. I'd rather die than be arrested."[10]

This depiction of Hardin's arrest aboard a train at Pensacola, Florida, appeared in the gunman's autobiography. (*The Life of John Wesley Hardin*, copyright 1896)

On August 28, 1877, John Wesley Hardin arrived in Austin, Texas. He recalled: "When we got to Austin, my guards learned that there was a tremendous crowd at the depot, and so they stopped the train and took a hack for the jail. The crowd at the depot learned of the move and broke for the jail. The hack just did manage to get there first, and they carried me bodily into the jail; so when the crowd arrived, they failed to see the great curiosity."[11]

One newspaper made light of Hardin's reputation, noting that "It is not the mere fact of Wes Hardin having killed twenty-six men that surprises people, but how he came to do it without being a successful physician. Maybe he read Eli Perkins's humorous lecture to his victims."[12]

On September 18, 1877, Comanche County Sheriff F. E. Wilson and a horde of deputies arrived in Austin to return Hardin, heavily shackled, to Comanche, where he would stand trial for the murder of Charles Webb.

Trial

The turnout for Hardin's homecoming in Comanche was equally impressive. One correspondent wrote:

> Everything is quiet at present. Cotton coming in rapidly — we have the only gin in this part of the country. The cotton crop is good considering the drouth, and we expect a good trade this fall and winter.
>
> Yesterday (Monday) about ten o'clock in the morning, the town was under some excitement, as well as interest, on learning that John Wesley Hardin was coming in town. The news spread like lightning and in a few seconds everybody had left their employment to get a glimpse of him. Crowds had gathered along the streets where he had to pass, eagerly waiting his arrival. (I must say that your correspondent was

among them.) At last they came, Sheriff Wilson and Major Griffeth, with twenty-two rangers accompanying him. He is now in jail, and it is well guarded. We do not apprehend any danger of a mob — everything is quiet at present.[13]

For all the accounts of Hardin's arrest — the *Victoria Advocate* splashed it across almost the entire front page — coverage of a great murder trial, THE STATE OF TEXAS VS No. 435 JOHN WESLEY HARDIN, is utterly disappointing. Transcripts don't exist, and newspaper accounts are sporadic at best. Hardin barely touched upon the trial in his autobiography, giving only two pages to the trial and appeal.

A grand jury had returned indictments against Hardin and Jim Taylor for Webb's murder on October 31, 1874. The indictment, based on three witnesses for the state, charged that Hardin and Taylor, "with pistols then and there loaded and charged with gunpowder and leaden balls; which said pistols the said John Wesley Hardin and James Taylor in their hands then and there had and held, then and there unlawfully feloniously and of their malice aforethought did shoot off, and discharge at, to, against, upon and into the body of the said Charles Webb, and the said John Wesley Hardin and James Taylor, with the leaden balls aforesaid, out of the guns aforesaid, then and there by force of the gunpowder aforesaid, by the said John Wesley Hardin and James Taylor shot off and discharged aforesaid, then and there unlawfully feloniously and of their malice aforethought did strike, penetrate and wound him, the said Charles Webb, giving to him, the said Charles Webb, then and there with the leaden balls aforesaid, in as aforesaid discharged and shot out of the pistols aforesaid by the said John Wesley Hardin & James Taylor, in and upon the body of him the said Charles Webb two mortal wounds, of which mortal wounds he the said Charles Webb then and there instantly died.

"And so the jurors aforesaid upon their oaths do say that the said John Wesley Hardin and James Taylor, him the said Charles Webb in the manner and by the means aforesaid feloniously and of their malice aforethought did kill and murder contrary to law and against the peace and dignity of the state."[14]

Foreman A. J. Jones signed the indictment.

By 1877 the aforesaid Jim Taylor was dead, so Hardin faced a jury of his peers alone. Comanche had first crack at the Texas hardcase, with murder indictments also reportedly against him in Freestone, Gonzales, Grimes, Hill, Hopkins, Navarro, Sabine, Titus, Trinity, and Wilson Counties as well, not to mention cattle-rustling charges. Hardin had thrown a wide loop, and he was only twenty-four years old.

He hired Samuel Henry Renick of Waco, Thomas Lewis Nugent of Stephenville, and W. S. J. Adams of Comanche for his defense, along with Comanche's G. R. Hart and Brenham's Abner Lipscomb. Leading the state's prosecution were district attorney N. R. Lindsey and county attorney John D. Stephens, assisted by Brownwood lawyers S. C. Buck and Colonel S.P. Burns.

The judge was James Richard Fleming of the 12th Judicial Court of Comanche. In addition to being a devout Methodist, the good judge also happened to be one of county attorney John Stephens's law partners in Comanche.

The trial began Friday, September 28, 1877.

Sporting a mustache and goatee, Hardin walked into court wearing a blue-gray suit, blue cravat, and rings on his fingers. The trial would last only two days, but those days would be long with testimony and arguments reaching well into the night. Fleming promptly called court to order, and the state announced it was ready to proceed. So did Hardin's attorneys, which caused mild surprise in the courtroom. Hardin was arraigned, the indictment was modified to note Jim Taylor's demise, and the defendant pleaded not guilty.

"More than half of the day was occupied in obtaining a jury," the *Galveston Daily News* reported, "but it is a remarkable fact that but eight peremptory challenges were made by the prisoner's counsel and four by the prosecuting attorneys, and yet it is doubtful if a fairer or more impartial jury could have been found in any county in the State to try John Wesley Hardin."[15]

What frustrates historians is that newspaper accounts did not identify any of the witnesses. Leon Metz notes that the prosecution called eight to ten witnesses, and that the defense brought two more to the stand. Among the witnesses later identified was William Cunningham, who said Charles Webb had arrested the son of a Mrs. Waldrip, and Cunningham heard Joe Hardin tell her they would take care of the deputy for her.

"The substance of the testimony," the *Galveston Daily News* reported, "was that Hardin and others of his party had been heard to utter threats against the deceased — his brother having remarked, when a party of them were together, that 'We will get away with them [Webb and others] at the proper time and place.'"[16]

Hardin told Taylor he had "gone back upon him" and said, "You knew I expected a difficulty." G. W. Talbot, whom Hardin owed money for a livery bill, apparently testified that when Webb approached the saloon where Hardin, Taylor, and others were waiting outside, Hardin asked Taylor, "Did you ever see anything working up finer in your life?"

When Webb walked past Hardin, the gunman asked him if he were the Brown County sheriff.

"No, I am the deputy sheriff," Webb answered.

"I understand you have papers for me," Hardin said.

Webb said he didn't know him, so Hardin introduced himself: "I am that d——d desperado, John Wesley Hardin. Now you know me."

The testimony basically follows the accounts Hardin gave to newspaper reporters after his arrest and arrival in Austin and later in his autobiography. Webb said he carried no arrest warrant for Hardin. The gunman became suspicious of what Webb held in his hands behind his back, and the deputy showed him a cigar.

"I have heard that you said that John Carnes, the sheriff of this county, is no man and no sheriff," Hardin said. Webb denied having ever said any such thing. Testimony then relates a different incident.

At this time Judge Thurmond, of Brownwood, who was standing in the street, called to Webb, saying, "come here Charlie," at which Hardin turned to Thurmond, saying, "you go on; we are attending to Charley now." Webb started to go to Thurmond, but was again detained by Hardin, who remarked: "You are not going away from me in that way." Webb then stepped back, remarking: "No, G— d—— you, I am not afraid of you," and drawing his pistol at the same time. The pistol fired accidentally as he drew it from the scabbard, and Hardin, Taylor and Dixon fired at the same time, their balls taking effect, Webb falling to the ground. Webb fired one shot after he fell, when

Taylor advanced upon him and shot him again, killing him instantly."[17]

"Hardin presented an indifferent, fearless countenance while the above testimony was being given, and when one important witness was on the stand, turned to him and gazed steadily in his face, with the evident purpose of looking him out of countenance," the *Daily News* said.[18]

In his autobiography, Hardin wrote: "The State tried to prove a conspiracy, but utterly failed in this, hence the prosecution ought to have fallen through. The State proved themselves that Charley Webb had fired at me twice before I drew my pistol, or that I drew and fired as he was shooting the second shot.

"The simple fact is that Charles Webb had really come over from his own county that day to kill me, thinking I was drinking and at a disadvantage. He wanted to kill me to keep his name, and he made his break on me like an assassin would. He fired his first shot at my vitals when I was unprepared, and who blames a man for shooting under such conditions."[19]

Accounts concur that Webb pulled and fired first, so prosecutor Stephens, who as a senator had been instrumental in getting the Legislature to put a $4,000 bounty on Hardin's head, likely knew he had to settle for a second-degree murder conviction and not capital murder. Hardin also pointed out that he was hurting even before the trial began. His key witnesses — notably brother Joe, cousin Bud Dixon, and pal Jim Taylor — were dead, many of them cut down by lynch mobs.

Perhaps the newspaper reporters said a fair jury had been seated, but Hardin suggested that six of those jurors had been implicated in the callous murder of Joe Hardin and the Dixon brothers.

Closing arguments began Friday night and continued Saturday, when District Attorney N. R. Lindsey made his statement. "His argument was a masterly effort," the *Galveston Daily News* noted, "and was commented on generally as reflecting the highest credit upon one so young in the profession. He was followed by other counsel representing the State and the defense."[20]

Arguments closed at eight o'clock that night, after which Fleming charged the jury. While the twelve men debated the testimony, some Texas Rangers and sheriff's deputies paced the courtroom's aisles while others stood guard in front of the jury room. One newspaper described the scene as "the flaring light of the candles gleaming upon their pistols and leading to a scene resembling a warlike appearance."[21]

After deliberating ninety minutes to three hours (accounts vary), the jury came out that night and announced a unanimous verdict:

> We the jury find the defendant guilty of murder in the second degree and assess his punishment at confinement in the penitentiary at hard labor for twenty-five years.
>
> D. L. DODDS, Foreman.[22]

The Galveston correspondent noted:

> Hardin was greatly disappointed in this verdict, but manifested no feeling in the court room, having been warned by an officer that such action on his part might have an influence on the crowd present dangerous to his safety. He wept bitterly after he was returned to jail, and complained that the jury had

been too hard upon him . . . . He indulged in several fits of weeping, and evidently felt that the punishment of death could not have been much worse than he is to receive.[23]

Immediate fears of a lynching rose, but nothing happened. Hardin's attorneys filed a motion for a new trial, which was rejected on Sunday. The next day Sheriff Wilson and twenty rangers commanded by Lieutenant N. O. Reynolds, took Hardin to the Travis County jail, where he would be for safe-keeping pending the appeals process.

"His removal has restored our village to its usual order and quiet," the Galveston correspondent concluded.[24]

While in the Austin jail, Hardin wrote a letter, dated April 1, 1878, to the Austin *Gazette* to plead his case.

Exceptions taken in my case at Comanche:

First _ The court required the defense to examine jurors before the state had finally passed upon them.

Second _ The court allowed witnesses to give evidence of threats made by parties not jointly indicted with me or present at the time of the difficulty.

Third _ The court allowed the state to introduce evidence of the escape of the defendant when they relied upon direct evidence of the killing.

Fourth _ The court amended on plan in bar to the second indictment on account of the pending of the first.

Fifth _ That there is a defect in the indictment: it does not state the time, place and where Webb died.

These exceptions, with a few more, are what I expect to have my case reversed on. It is true the state of Texas has spent many dollars to convict me; but for a few dollars would the state of Texas rob me of my rights and privileges? I hope not. I have been compared to the beasts of the forest; but, my dear readers, I am a human being, a native of the great state of Texas, and all I ask is law and justice, which I hope I will yet get.[25]

The law didn't side with Hardin and turned down his appeal that June. On September 20 Lieutenant Reynolds arrived in Austin with twenty rangers to escort Hardin back to Comanche for his sentencing. Shackled, the gunman arrived without incident to appear before Judge Fleming on September 28. In his statement, Hardin claimed self-defense and said his conviction was unjust.

Fleming sentenced Hardin to twenty-five years of hard labor at the state penitentiary in Huntsville. The gunman was taken to the Comanche County jail before being transported to the prison along with blacksmith John Maston, who had been convicted of attempted murder and sentenced to two years at Huntsville, and two other convicts. Maston, Hardin said, later killed himself in prison.

He arrived at Huntsville on October 5, a five-foot-nine, one-hundred-sixty-pound twenty-five-year-old, Convict Number 7109. Huntsville would be his home for the next fifteen years.

Aftermath

First assigned to the wheelwright's shop, Hardin didn't plan on making Huntsville home for very long. He and several other inmates began tunneling seventy-five yards from the wheelwright's shop to the armory, where the prison guards would store their weapons before retiring for supper. It was a bold plan. Once they captured the guns, the prisoners would take over the prison, force the guards and officials to surrender, and then free every prisoner who wanted to escape — except rapists.

They reached the armory on November 1 but still had to cut through five twenty-four-inch-thick brick walls with saw bits, chisels, and other contraband. On November 20 the prisoners were ready to cut through the pine floor and take the guns, but several squeamish lifers rushed to the superintendent's office and squealed. Hardin and nine others were arrested, and Hardin was put in a dark cell, shackled to a ball and chain, and given only bread and water for fifteen days.

Once out of the hole, Hardin was assigned to work in a factory with turnkey John Williams, and Hardin concocted another escape plan. He would make keys to all the cells on his row at the factory as well as keys to the outer gates. On the day after Christmas, Hardin gave the keys to Williams to see if they worked. Williams returned and said they "worked like a charm," so Hardin planned on departing Huntsville that night. What he didn't realize was that Williams was an informer, and instead of escaping that night, Hardin found himself jumped in his cell by twenty guards, tied up, flogged thirty-nine times until "my sides and back were beaten into jelly," forced to march across the snow to another building, and kept for three days in another dark cell without food.

Freed from the hole on the fourth day, Hardin, suffering from a high fever and unable to walk, was taken to another cell, where he stayed for thirty days.

Other schemes also failed. He worked in various shops and finally was making quilts when he was given permission to read after finishing his assignments. By 1882 Hardin had studied theology and had been president of the inmates' debating society and superintendent of Sunday school. In 1885 he began studying law. The Texas hardcase had become a model inmate. The man who had tried to get out of prison any way he could now sought a legal recourse to obtain freedom.

Hardin lost his wife of twenty years when Jane, likely suffering from tuberculosis, died on November 6, 1892, at age thirty-five. She left three children. On January 1, 1893, Hardin filed a request for pardon to Governor James S. Hogg. The celebrated gunman, once Texas's most wanted fugitive, had the backing of most of the newspapers and many residents. Hogg agreed, granting Hardin a full pardon and restoring him "to full citizenship with the right of suffrage."[26]

On February 17, 1894, John Wesley Hardin left the Texas State Penitentiary a free man. He was forty years old. Two days later he arrived in Gonzales, where he was admitted to the state bar on July 21. He left his children and law practice in November for Kerrville. On January 9, 1895, he married fifteen-year-old Carolyn "Callie" Lewis in London, Texas — one legend goes that Hardin won Callie from her father in a poker game — but had dropped the teen off at her parents within a couple of weeks. Apparently they never filed for divorce or annulment, and Hardin drifted west alone to El Paso.

In this dusty border city of thirteen thousand — a gunfighters mecca — Hardin hung up his shingle at 200 1/2 El Paso in the Wells Fargo building and started practicing law. He had a few clients, but business tapered off, and Hardin returned to the gambling dens and saloons. He wasn't a good loser. On May 1, 1895, he grabbed the pot on an Acme Saloon poker table after dropping a load of cash and walked away. His reputation remained intact, and no one tried to stop him.

At the Gem Saloon the next night, he pulled a Colt Thunderer after losing money in a craps game and took back what he had lost. He was arrested on May 6 and charged with carrying a gun, gambling, and armed robbery of the Gem Saloon. He made bail on the robbery charge and was granted a continuance until October 1. He was found guilty of the two other charges and fined a total of $35. His confiscated Colt revolver (and other weapons) were not returned.

Hardin drank heavily. He gambled and lost. He consorted with his mistress, one Beulah McRose.

On August 19, 1895, Hardin and Constable John Selman got into an argument on the streets. Apparently Selman's son had arrested McRose for carrying a pistol, and she had been convicted. Hardin told Selman: "You've got a son that is a bastardly, cowardly son of a bitch."

"Which one?" Selman asked.

Hardin answered, and Selman responded: "Hardin, there is no man on earth that can talk about my children like that without fighting, you cowardly son of a bitch."

When Hardin said he was unarmed, Selman said: "Go and get your gun. I am armed."

Hardin shot back: "I'll go and get a gun and when I meet you I'll meet you smoking and make you pull like a wolf around the block."[27]

The two men left. Hardin went to hit the bottle and gamble. At ten o'clock he was shooting dice in the Acme Saloon with Henry Brown, a grocer. Selman, brooding, planted himself in front of the saloon. An hour later E. L. Shackleford, a friend of Selman, entered the saloon. Apparently Shackleford went in and out of the Acme several times, possibly reporting Hardin's activities and state of inebriation to Selman. On the final time, Selman followed Shackleford into the saloon.

Hardin had just rolled the dice and told Brown: "Brown, you've got four sixes to beat."

Selman had already drawn his gun, and he sent one .45-caliber slug into Hardin's head. Two other bullets struck Hardin in his right breast and right arm. Selman said: "I noticed that Hardin watched me very closely as we went in. When he thought my eye was off him he made a break for his gun in his hip pocket and I immediately pulled my gun and began shooting. I shot him in the head first as I had been informed that he wore a steel breast plate."[28]

Selman's son ran inside, grabbed his father's arm, and said, "He is dead. Don't shoot any more." John Wesley Hardin had died instantly. "I was not drunk at the time," Selman said, "but was crazy mad at the way he had insulted me."[29]

John Selman was indicted for murder and brought to trial in El Paso in February 1896. A hung jury (which voted 10-2 for acquittal) resulted in a mistrial, and a new trial was set for the next year. The retrial became moot, however, on Easter Sunday, April 5, 1896.

That's when a drunken John Henry Selman met Deputy United States Marshal George Scarborough in an El Paso alley at four in the morning. What happened next and why have been debated, but insults flew, and bullets followed. Hit four times, Selman died in surgery at Sisters Hospital that afternoon. Scarborough would be charged but acquitted of Selman's murder only to die during surgery on April 5, 1900, in Deming, New Mexico Territory, after being shot in a leg while chasing rustlers.

Selman was buried in Concordia Cemetery, not far from where John Wesley Hardin, Texas's greatest gunfighter, had been laid to rest.

Chapter Notes

Primary sources: *John Wesley Hardin: Dark Angel of Texas* (University of Oklahoma Press, 1996) by Leon Metz; *The Life of John Wesley Hardin as Written by Himself* (University of Oklahoma Press, 1961) by John Wesley Hardin; *The Law Comes to Texas: The Texas Rangers 1870-1901* (State House Press, 1999) by Frederick Wilkins; *The Letters of John Wesley Hardin* (Eakin Press, 2001) compiled by Roy and Jo Ann Stamps; *Triggernometry: A Gallery of Gunfighters* (University of Oklahoma Press, 1996) by Eugene Cunningham; *300 Years in Victoria County* (Victoria Advocate Publishing Co., date??) edited by Roy Grimes; *The Handbook of Texas Online*; Comanche County District Clerk holdings; and various 1877-78 editions of the *Galveston Daily News*, *Galveston Weekly News*, *Dallas Weekly Herald*, *Dallas Daily Herald*, and *Victoria Advocate*.

1. T. N. McKinney memoir, American Life Histories, Federal Writers' Project, 1936-1940.

2. Hardin, John Wesley. *The Life of John Wesley Hardin as Written by Himself*, p. 6.

3. Hardin, p. 13.

4. Hardin, pp. 45-46.

5. Hardin, pp. 83-84.

6. Hardin, p. 84.

7. Dialogue and details from Hardin, pp. 92-93.

8. *Victoria Advocate*, September 8, 1877.

9. Ibid.

10. Ibid.

11. Hardin, p. 122.

12. *Galveston Daily News*, August 29, 1877.

13. *Dallas Weekly Herald*, September 29, 1877.

14. Grand Jury Foreman charge, Comanche County District Clerk records.

15. *Galveston Daily News*, October 7, 1877. Reprinted in the *Galveston Weekly News* October 15, 1877.

16. Ibid.

17. Ibid.

18. Ibid.

19. Hardin, p. 124.

20. *Galveston Daily News*, October 7, 1877. Reprinted in the *Galveston Weekly News* October 15, 1877.

21. *Weatherford Exponent*, October 13, 1877, quoted in Leon Metz, *John Wesley Hardin: Dark Angel of Texas*, p. 180.

22. *Galveston Daily News*, October 7, 1877. Reprinted in the *Galveston Weekly News* October 15, 1877.

23. Ibid.

24. Ibid.

25. *Dallas Daily Herald*, April 13, 1878.

26. Proclamation by the Governor of the State of Texas No. 3029, Comanche County District Clerk records.

27. *El Paso Daily Herald*, August 20, 1895.

28. Ibid.

29. Ibid.

"Hanging is my favorite way of dying"

Trial of Bill Longley

«————————————————»

Giddings, Texas, 1877

Prelude*

Historians have had a difficult time separating the truth and legends of William P. Longley, partly because of Bill Longley himself. While awaiting trial and sentence, he penned a number of autobiographical letters published in several Texas newspapers, but "Bloody Bill/Wild Bill/Big Bill" Longley was one to stretch the truth a mite, especially regarding his own accomplishments. As the *Galveston Daily News* reported:

"It is thought by many who have read the accounts of his escapes, his dangers and his desperate assaults, that there is a good deal of fiction in his narratives, but others, who have known him from his boyhood, assert that it would be a difficult task to exaggerate the reckless daring of the man, and his capacities for carrying into execution the murder of his enemies in the most cruel and heartless manner."[1]

A contemporary of noted shootists such as Cullen Baker, John Wesley Hardin, Ben Thompson, and King Fisher, Longley lived — and died — during the heyday of Texas gunfighters. Less than a century after his death, during the heyday of TV Westerns, a series loosely inspired on his life hit the CBS airwaves. From 1958-60, Rory Calhoun starred as Big Bill Longley in *The Texan*, but it's fair to say that the television hero, who went around saving good folk from bad men, was a far cry from the real William Longley, a racist, ill-tempered, and possibly a psychopathic killer.

Wild Bill Longley was a good guy in the 1950s TV series *The Texan*, even inspiring this 1959 Dell Comic. In real life, Longley was no hero. (Author's Collection)

After he was arrested in Louisiana and returned to Texas — without the benefit of extradition — Longley was said to have killed thirty-two men, and the gunman would casually add, "Oh, I killed lots of niggers and Mexicans, whom I did not count."[2] In the most thorough biography of Longley, *Bloody Bill Longley*, author Rick Miller pares down that number to approximately five, and Longley himself would later admit he had exaggerated his kills, telling Sheriff James Madison Brown "that he had really killed but eight men, six whites and two colored; though he had shot several others who did not die."[3]

Thirty-two, eight, or five, William Longley would be brought to justice for one slaying, the cold-blooded murder of Wilson Anderson on March 31, 1875.

William Preston Longley entered this world on October 6, 1851, in Austin County, Texas, the sixth child of Campbell Longley and Pennsylvania native Sarah Ann Henry Longley. Campbell Longley had been born in 1816 in Tennessee but, like many Tennesseans, migrated southwest to Texas, where he joined the Texas army in 1836 and later settled in Austin County. When Bill Longley was two years old, the family moved to Evergreen, in Washington County, where he received a rural education typical of farmers of the period. Bill Longley could read and write and was baptized, he said, at age twelve.

Too young to serve in the Civil War, Longley nevertheless had strong Confederate sympathies. Contemporary newspaper accounts say Longley became a hero-worshiper, listening in awe to the stories told by Confederate veterans, and by the end of the war, Longley had been transformed into an unreconstructed rebel and, like many Texans of the time, an unrepentant racist.

"It was immediately after the late war that he entered upon that course of crime unparalleled which surpassed the darkest deeds of Murrell, and finally led him to the foot of the gallows," the *St. Louis Daily Globe-Democrat* said of Longley. "On the surrender of the Confederate armies, in 1865, the almost juvenile William, with a young man named McCowan, volunteered to disarm some negroes in the vicinity of Evergreen."[4]

Legend has it that in 1866, the fifteen-year-old Longley took a train to Houston and started down the owlhoot trail. According to the story, a black policeman confronted Longley and a white friend on a cold, rainy night. Longley's pal killed the man with a knife, and Longley took the slain man's sidearm, a percussion-style Dance .44 revolver.

A 20th-century replica of the Civil War era Dance .44. The Texas-made pistol, according to legend, was Longley's first revolver. (Author's Collection)

The Dance had been made for the Confederacy by Texas-based J. H. Dance & Company and was popular during the Civil War. A hybrid 1848 Colt Dragoon .44 and 1851 Colt Navy .36, the flat-framed six-shooter was constructed of iron, with a brass trigger guard and backstrap and walnut grips but without recoil shields. The .44 Dance (.36-caliber models were also produced) usually had an eight-inch barrel and weighed three pounds, six ounces. Fewer than 400 models were made between 1862 and 1865, but the Dance revolvers remained popular. Longley reportedly carried a Dance .44 with the serial number of 4.

The young Longley became a crack shot with his new revolver.

Another story has it that a black man rode through the town of Old Evergreen cussing out each white man he passed, but when he made the mistake of insulting Longley's father, young Bill Longley shot the man dead. That could be hogwash, but it could also be true. It is known, however, that in December 1868 Longley, McCowan (or McKeown, or McKowen), and James Gilmore waylaid three former slaves on their way to visit friends and kinfolk in Austin County. One of the slaves, Green Evans, was killed when he tried to escape, but the other two men got away. Bill Longley was later identified as one of the killers, and he took flight.

Longley said he worked for a while as a cowboy for stockman John Reagan in Karnes County, Texas, for several months before deciding to ride home. While passing through the settlement of Yorktown, Longley had the misfortune, if you believe his story, to be mistaken for another Texas outlaw, Charlie Taylor. A posse of soldiers from the Sixth Ohio Cavalry took after Longley in a chase described by the *St. Louis Daily Globe-Democrat*:

There was a running fight. The soldiers fired forty and the murderer five shots without effect. One of the cavalry rode so close to the desperado that the hammer of the latter's pistol caught in the lappel [sic] of the soldier's overcoat. Pulling back the weapon it was discharged, the ball entering the soldier's body, killing him almost instantly. This murder occurred during the period of reconstruction, when Texas was under martial law. Hearing that $1,000 reward was out for him, the young cut-throat fled to his old haunts in Washington County. Remaining at his old home a short time he, by the advice of his father, left for Arkansas.[5]

That story is also uncorroborated, as well as Longley's alleged exploits with Cullen Montgomery Baker. A Tennessean by birth, Baker and his family moved to Texas in 1839 and settled in Cass County. If Baker and Longley did become associates, it was a match made in Hell, for both men were heavy drinkers, bigots, and quick-tempered. Both became sanitized and glamorized a century later, Longley in *The Texan* TV series and Baker in the popular Louis L'Amour novel *The First Fast Draw*.

In reality, Baker had killed two men by the outbreak of the Civil War. He enlisted in Morgan's Regimental Cavalry in Jefferson, Texas, in November 1861, but apparently deserted then joined the Fifteenth Texas Cavalry in Linden in February 1862 and was discharged a year later with an undisclosed sickness. After the war Baker and his second wife settled in Cass County, and when his wife died on March 1, 1866, Cullen Baker became depressed, drinking, the legends go, whiskey laced with strychnine.

Another unreconstructed rebel, Baker and his gang terrorized members of the Union army, the Freedmen's Bureau, and white and black settlers in Texas and Arkansas. Baker's gang is said to have murdered at least two agents in the Freedmen's Bureau, as well as numerous blacks. Baker wasn't limited to tormenting the newly freed blacks. He hated schoolteacher Thomas Orr and once tried to hang the prominent area politician, but the Orr-Baker feud had little to do with politics. Two months after Baker's second wife died, Baker had proposed to his wife's sister, Bell Foster, but Foster spurned the gunman and married Orr.

By December 1868 the Baker gang had disbanded, and the outlaw went home to Cass County. On January 6, 1869, Baker's reign of terror ended when Thomas Orr and a group of vigilantes caught up with Baker at his home, where they killed him and a companion.

Longley said he met Baker while traveling through Arkansas. In Fayette County, Longley joined an associate of Baker's named Johnson and spent the night at Johnson's home when vigilantes raided the house. Johnson and Longley were tied up and hanged from a tree. The *Galveston Daily News* said:

> One of the party to make sure work of their mission fired three shots into Johnson's body and two at Longley, one of which was prevented from inflicting a dangerous wound by the bullet striking a belt containing gold that he had secured around his body. The other shot struck the rope by which he was hanging and severing two of the cords, the strands soon gave way under his weight, and he fell to the ground before death ensued. A little brother of Johnson's followed the lynchers, and coming up to the scene of the tragedy about the time Longley fell, he cut the rope from his neck and restored him to life. Johnson was dead when cut down. After this narrow escape he lay for

several days concealed in the woods and was sustained in the meantime by the family of Johnson.[6]

Yeah, right. It reads like pure Longley lies, but the paper went on to say: "Cullen Baker visited him in his ambush, and after several talks over the matter enlisted him in his gang of outlaws. He served for some months with this gang, which was principally engaged in robbing government trains and in murdering union sympathizers and negroes."[7]

It's probably nothing more than a Tall Texas Tale, but whether or not he teamed up with the notorious Cullen Baker, Longley was doing his share of killing. In 1869 and 1870 Longley and his brother-in-law, John W. Wilson, apparently murdered a black man named Brice in Bastrop County and a black woman, whom they may have also raped. Reconstruction government placed a reward for the two fiends, and shortly after Wilson somehow met his death in Brazos County in 1870, Longley fled north.

If you buy into Longley's stories, he had a series of murderous adventures on his trek north, including this incident involving an army soldier in a Leavenworth, Kansas, saloon.

"Where are you from?" inquired the soldier.

"Texas."

"I would be ashamed to tell it."

"Why?"

"The Texans are all thieves," answered the soldier.

"It is a lie, and you'd better hush up on Texas!" rejoined the desperado.

"I tell you," continued the soldier, "the Texans are all thieves, and there isn't a virtuous woman in the State!"

These were the last words he ever uttered. Longley shot and instantly killed him, and escaped in double-quick order.[8]

In 1870 the wannabe-rebel did an about-face when he enlisted in the United States Cavalry but quickly deserted and was captured and sentenced to two years at Camp Stambaugh, a post established in 1870 between Atlantic City and the Oregon Trail in Wyoming Territory. Paroled after six months and returned to his troop, Longley deserted again two years later. He said he lived with the Shoshone Indians for a while — hogwash, most historians say — before drifting south for Texas, where he cowboyed again and killed a few other men.

In any event, Longley was in Kerr County, Texas, when he was arrested by Mason County Sheriff J. J. Finney and transported to Austin, where Finney would collect the reward. When Finney received no money from the government, a relative of Longley is said to have given the sheriff a bribe, and Longley conveniently escaped, taking to the owlhoot trail once more with a fresh horse and brace of pistols.

Again Longley drifted, but fate brought him to the home of his uncle, Caleb Longley, late in 1874. Uncle Caleb met Longley at the front gate, crying, embracing the gunman, and pointing to a grave, sobbing how it wasn't fair that Little Cale Longley lay dead while his murderer lived only a mile away. Little Cale, about the same age as Bill Longley, had been on a drinking binge with Wilson Anderson, a childhood friend of Longley's, at Giddings when his horse bolted, and Little Cale's head slammed into a low branch of an oak tree, smashing his skull. That's how Wilson Anderson explained the tragedy, but the boy's father and family said Anderson had done the smashing himself, using a club to brain poor Little Cale. The law saw it Wilson Anderson's way, and thus Little Cale was buried and Wilson Anderson was free.

That wasn't fair, and Uncle Caleb begged his nephew to kill Wilson Anderson before he left. At first Longley would have nothing to do with it, suggesting that Uncle Caleb or Little Cale's brothers should do any avenging, but he finally relented after Uncle Caleb mentioned that Wilson Anderson also said William Preston Longley was a low-down horse thief and had threatened to kill the shootist himself.

On March 31, 1875, Longley, armed with a shotgun, and his younger brother, Jim, left their uncle's farm. Nearing the Anderson farm, Longley told his brother to stay put and rode down to where Anderson was plowing a field. Apparently Jim Longley had not been informed of his brother's murderous designs, but he suspected something and rode after him just in time to witness the murder. There have been several accounts of what happened, but in all of them, Bill Longley killed Wilson Anderson with the shotgun, and the two brothers fled. In most versions Longley fired both charges from the shotgun with the second one proving fatal. Wilson Anderson had been plowing a cotton field at the time and was not armed. Another story has it that as Anderson lay dying he asked Longley why he had shot him, and the killer answered coldly, "Just for luck."

On May 10, 1875, a grand jury in Lee County returned murder indictments against Bill and Jim Longley, and Governor Richard Coke offered a reward of $175 for the arrest of each brother. By the end of August, Jim Longley had been arrested and the reward for Bill was up to $250.

The Longley cases were severed in December, and Jim Longley was tried for murder on May 26, 1876. The jury's deliberation was quick, and Jim Longley was found not guilty.

Meanwhile, Bill Longley continued to drift and kill. George Thomas became a victim in McLennan County in November 1875, and William "Lou" Shroyer, alias Lon Sawyer, died in January 1876. In the latter gunfight, the caps on Longley's percussion pistol "got all wet and would not ignite," so he grabbed a "cowboy rifle," loaded his "good pistol," and kept up the fight. Shroyer fired fourteen shots and Longley eighteen; Longley survived and Shroyer did not.

One month after Shroyer's death, Longley was arrested in Delta County, Texas. After six days in jail, he escaped by burning the jail. Longley had been sharecropping for and feuding with the Reverend William R. Lay during his time in Delta County, and on June 13, 1876, he killed the minister while he was milking a cow. Lay lived long enough, though, to identify his murderer. With a price of $500 now on his head, Bill Longley fled to Louisiana, where he would be captured almost one year later. He was described as standing six feet tall with black hair and whiskers, a spare build, somewhat stooped shoulders, weighing one hundred and fifty pounds, and having unmistakable piercing black eyes.

In Nacogdoches County, Sheriff Milton Mast became suspicious of a man working on W. T. Gamble's farm near Keatchie. The lawman wrote Texas authorities, and upon being convinced the farm hand was in fact Bill Longley, Mast, two deputies and constable June Courtney planned to capture the fugitive going by the name "Bill Jackson." In early June 1877 they arrived at the Gamble farm, saying they were chasing a fugitive black man and needed Longley's help. Longley agreed to help, but as he went to open the gate, Mast and a deputy

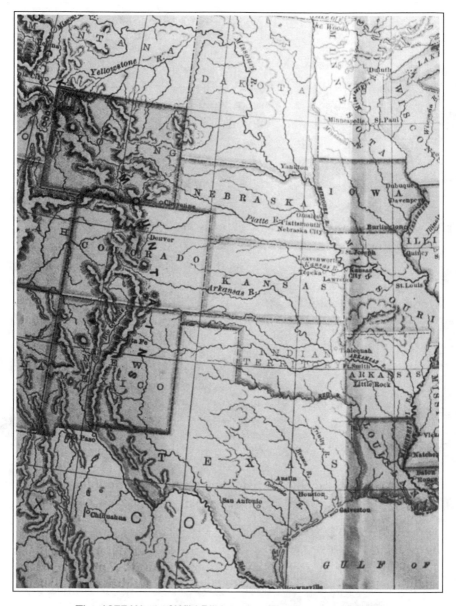

The 1877 West of Wild Bill Longley. The gunman roamed
much of the West during his life. (Author's Collection)

drew their weapons and Courtney stuck a revolver barrel in Longley's back.

The outlaw cursed the lawmen, who handcuffed him, tossed him into a wagon, and hauled across the Texas border, fourteen miles east. On June 9, 1877, Bloody Bill Longley was placed in the Lee County jail in Giddings, Texas, to await his trial for the murder of Wilson Anderson. Apparently Longley felt good about his chances in this trial and was pleased not to have been taken to Delta County, Texas, where he figured he would have surely been hanged for the murder of the Reverend William Lay.

Trial

While waiting in the Lee County jail, Sheriff James Madison Brown allowed Longley to write to his heart's content, providing the sheriff read the letters before they were posted. Longley filled many pages, writing his father as well as various newspapers, including the *Giddings Tribune* and *Galveston Daily News*. On August 1, the *Galveston Daily News* noted:

Bill Longley has concluded his history of his life and adventures in the Giddings *Tribune*. He boasts of many murders and other crimes, and professes to expect to be hung. He will doubtless expect to play the hero, if not the Christian, under the gallows. There is no accounting for taste even in the most serious affairs, and some men may be like the fellow who took pride in boasting that his grandfather had spoken to the largest crowd ever assembled in the county and then given his life for the good of his country, the fact being simply that he was hung with the usual ceremonies. Nevertheless, the *Tribune* publishes a card from

Sheriff Brown, of Lee county, stating that hereafter no one will be allowed to visit Bill Longley in the jail. He says Longley will be heavily and securely ironed, and guards will be perpetually on watch. Longley will hardly be disappointed in his professed belief that he can not cheat the gallows this time. It may save the county future expense if a few of his confederates would attempt a rescue and are shot in the meantime.[9]

His trial date was scheduled for August 24, 1877, and Alabama native Samuel R. Kenada became Longley's attorney. In his mid- to late-thirties, Kenada had passed the bar only in March 1876 and had never tried a capital murder case. In a letter dated October 11, 1877, Longley explained his reason for hiring Kenada (although some historians suggest the lawyer had been appointed):

My father was threatened with death if he assisted in the least, and I was not allowed to receive letters or forward any, and Sam Kenada came to the jail to see a man that he was defending, and I employed him for the pitiful sum of $50, which was all I could raise from my own resources. I was not allowed to talk to him privately. He came back to the jail the second time, and the jailer [attacked?] him, and he came no more. I saw him no more until inside the bar.[10]

Meanwhile, the sheriff of Delta County wanted Longley to stand trial for the murder of pastor Lay, but Lee County claimed dibs on the gunman. The trial was postponed until September 3, at which time Sheriff Brown was to produce a *venire facias* of thirty-six potential jurors.

Captured! Bill Longley is flanked by Bill Burrows and Sheriff Milton Mast.
(Western History Collections, University of Oklahoma Library)

Presiding over the trial was Judge Ezekiel B. Turner. Born in 1825 in Putney, Vermont, Turner studied and later practiced law in Michigan before moving to Texas in 1853. A Republican, Turner was appointed U.S. attorney for the Western District of Texas in 1866 but resigned to take the position of the state's attorney general. He later served as district judge in Lampasas before being elected the Sixteenth Judicial District's judge in 1876.

Thirty-year-old Seth Shepard, helped by law partners C. C. Garrett and N. A. Rector, would prosecute Longley for the state. Shepard, a Confederate veteran, had received his law degree in 1868 and practiced in Brenham in Washington County. On Monday, September 3, the trial began.

Longley recalled: "They carried me to the court house chained hand and foot. They had 30 armed men with shotguns inside the bar all the time with their guns pointed toward me, almost to the act of firing."[11] A report in the *Galveston Daily News* on September 4 corroborated Longley's statement: "Longley's shackles are now being removed. Sheriff Brown has summoned a numerous guard of resolute men, who are well armed with shot-guns and six-shooters. The court-house is densely packed and interest intense; the concourse is the largest ever in attendance upon court at this place. Longley exhibits or affects exuberant spirits."[12]

Kenada filed a motion for a continuance because a defense witness, William Hayes of Uvalde County, had not been located, but the young lawyer could not adequately explain the importance of Hayes's testimony, so Judge Turner denied the motion. Shepard then announced that the state was ready for trial, the clerk read the indictment, and William Preston Longley pleaded not guilty. Recalled Longley: "The judge ordered the irons taken off, when they brought the blacksmith inside the bar and cut them. When court would adjourn at noon or night, they would rivet the irons on me again right in the bar. I believe if I had raised up on my feet they would have shot me into doll rags. I must say that I never saw as many contemptible, dirty cowards in one crowd before in my life. When one of them would happen to get close to me — and me chained, too — he would become so excited his teeth would chatter like he had an ague."[13]

The jury included mostly farmers and stock raisers. Although the *Galveston Daily News* reported that "Several days may be required to obtain a jury,"[14] the twelve men were seated on the first day, after which Judge Turner adjourned the court until 8:30 a.m. September 4.

Transcripts have not been discovered, if they still survive, and newspaper accounts are few and far between. The main prosecution witness was Wash Harris, who swore that Longley told him he had killed Wilson Anderson. Anderson's widow said she saw the Longley brothers riding away after the murder. Longley's Uncle Caleb and his wife were hostile witnesses for the state, forced to testify under oath that their nephew had admitted to killing Wilson Anderson. Other witnesses corroborated previous testimony, and Sheriff James Madison Brown identified a letter Longley had written in which he admitted killing Anderson.

Longley had trouble presenting any witnesses on his behalf. One man he wanted to take the stand couldn't. Joseph Hemphill had been arrested in Giddings in August and charged with the shooting death of a man named Holligan in Bastrop County. As far as the rest of the trial is concerned, Longley wrote to an "eminent criminal lawyer in Richmond," and the *Galveston Daily News* published the letter:

Well, Kenada made a very short talk to the jury, and asked them to not give me more than imprisonment for life and walked off. That was the last I saw of him. Then Seth Sheppard got up and gave me a blast, and bemoaned me to the lowest pitch, and said that I had committed many dastardly and cowardly murders, and he thought that I certainly ought to die. He was a volunteer lawyer against me — he told me himself that he volunteered his services, though he said the citizens told him if he did not do it they would take me in daylight and hang me.

I am not able to tell you hardly what disadvantage it was for Kenada to abandon me when he did, because I am so unacquainted with law that I do not know what harm it did me. No one ever made a motion for a new trial. Sir, I was even ignorant of such a thing as a new trial, for I never was tried before by civil law. When Kenada left me in the bar, he whispered and told me they would hang me in spite of hell — that is his words — if not by law, they would kill me before I got to jail. I was not the least excited because I expected to be killed at any minute. I just thought to myself if God has drawed off from me they will certainly kill me, but I thought to myself, just let them kill. If I was only guilty of one cowardly trick in my whole life I would not care if they did kill me, but they can not say that I am, in truth. All in the world they have against me is that they are afraid of me.

You ask if there was any statement of facts written out by my lawyer or the attorney for the State. Do you mean proved by my witnesses? Kenada never wrote anything. He never had the State's witnesses put under the rules, but no one ever did swear that they saw me kill Anderson. Nothing was positive — only a letter that Jim Brown said he received from me, and he swore to it. There have been ten or twelve letters written to me in that county with my name signed to them, and I never wrote one of them; and as to my witnesses, I had three summoned. One of them was impeached without a cause, and another came to me and told me that he would be mobbed if he swore the truth in my case — and he was a good friend to me — and I told him I would let him off for his own good; and the third one was not there at all. So I had no witnesses at all. One fellow swore a lie — he swore that I met him and three other men, and told him that I killed Anderson; and the state had all four of them summoned, and three of them swore that they did not hear me say one word about Anderson, and these three were all respectable citizens of Lee county, and the one that swore that I told them this was a man by the name of Wash Harris, who had been indicted in Caldwell county for cattle stealing in twenty or thirty cases, and they wrote down his evidence and never noticed the three others, and Harris was a relative of Anderson's.

(Wash Harris, by the way, was not related to Wilson Anderson, and it's unclear if he was ever accused of cattle rustling.)

Longley continued:

My lawyer took no bill of exceptions to the rulings of the judge. The testimony against me was not positive. I have stated all that amounted to anything in the above. I don't know how the jury was impaneled —

whether fair or not. The jury was just as prejudiced as they could be. One of them was a Dutchman by the name of ——, that my father and several other citizens had whipped about twenty-five years ago for hog-stealing, and I am satisfied that all of them were concerned in a mob that came to the jail about one month before court and tried to get the jailer to give them the keys. The only way he could get rid of them was to tell them if I was not convicted that they might have me after court. I heard the conversation and know nearly all of them. It was about one o'clock at night. Jim Brown was not there and when they found that I knew them they were determined to kill me. The man that summoned the jury was an enemy of mine. I don't know whether the jury separated during the trial or not; I never thought of that even. And I don't know of any misconduct of the jury, only they were very unconcerned while Kenada was speaking, and would laugh very heartily at him. Sometimes some of them were reading papers, and others were engaged in conversation with some of the guards in a low tone. One of them looked at me and gritted his teeth at me while Sheppard was speaking. The jury only stayed out about one hour. The verdict was written on paper and handed to the District Clerk by the foreman, and he read it. They started right to jail with me. Kenada was not in the room. One of the jury men was heard to say: "Boys, was not that done up all right? Let us have something to drink on that."[15]

After a short deliberation, foreman Fred Wade announced that the jury had reached a unanimous verdict and found William

P. Longley guilty of first-degree murder. A week later Longley was sentenced to death by hanging. The gunman said:

I was perfectly cool, but I knew of nothing that I could do, and if I had they would not have let me stay there to do it, and there was no one to do anything for me. Every body seemed joyful and well pleased about it. One fellow by the name of ——— came to the jail after the sentence was pronounced and began tantalizing me, and I told him he had the advantage of me, and he said, "Yes, you G-d d—n son of a b—. I have a notion to blow your d—n brains out right now," and drew his pistol and put it through the grates where I was chained to the wall. I pulled open my bosom and told him, "You cowardly scoundrel, shoot." Well, it is no use to tell you this. I could tell you a great deal more, but I will not do it now. My lawyer did not try to move the trial at all. I do not know who fixed up the appeal, nor what evidence was written down — they had it all to themselves.

When I went back to the jail I sat down and wrote to the judge and told him how I felt about it, and that I wanted to appeal, and that I hoped his honor would consider my fix and grant it to me. The man that gave him the letter said he cried when he read it, and when the judge passed the sentence on me, I told him I did not believe I had a fair trial, and that I wanted to appeal the case. He remarked that the law gave me that privilege, and he would have to grant it, and I heard him tell lawyer Sheppard to take charge of it, as I had no lawyer, and fix it up, and that is all I know about it. There was no evidence written down while the trial was going on. It was a surprise to them all when I got an appeal.

I was then threatened by a mob very strong, and the judge ordered Jim Brown to take me to Galveston jail; and you may know that I am very glad of it, for I am treated like a man here, not like a dog. Well, the transcript has not come yet, but when it does I will send it to you if you want to see it. I would like to have you[r] aid, but I do not know how much money I can raise, but if you can send me word that you can take it for then I can tell you, and if I can possibly raise it. I will do it, for I would rather have you than any one in the State, because I have more confidence in you than any other lawyer I know, and if you do take my case and lose it I will be perfectly satisfied, for if you lose it anyone else would too. If you had had it at first they never would have done what they did, but now it is in such a bad fix it may be hard to manage, but if I must hang I intend to hang like a man, but there is one thing I do know, and that is certain, and that is, every one of them fellows has got to die some day as well as me, and I am going to try to meet my God in peace, and I hope the good Lord will forgive them too, for if I don't get a new trial that jury has murdered me in colder blood than ever I did a man, and I have never harmed one of them in no way in my life, and the great God of heaven knows I have not. If they had given me a fair trial it would not have been so bad but I had no showing on earth — they had just as well went and killed me in jail.

Your friend until death, W. P. LONGLEY.[16]

The joyous reaction to Longley's conviction and death sentence was not limited to Giddings. The *Dallas Daily Herald* noted: "Bill Longley writes from the Galveston jail to the Nacogdoches News a letter, in which he says that the witnesses swore bushels of lies against him, wants twenty dollars to buy some of the filthy mud, gets sarcastic and says his business confines him to his office. Would like to be out to tackle a quart of liquor, etc. He will get out and off to a strange land, materially aided by a scaffold and a twisted piece of hemp."[17] And the *Victoria Advocate* noted: "The notorious ruffian, Longley, who boasts of the blood he had shed, was tried for murder at Giddings, Lee county, last week. The jury, after a short absence, returned a verdict of murder, and Longley will expiate his many crimes on the scaffold."[18]

Now secured in the Galveston jail, Longley continued to write friends and newspapers while awaiting a ruling from the Court of Appeals. Longley was represented by Bellville attorney Jacob H. Catlin. Perhaps Longley felt he had a reasonable chance for a new trial or at least having his death sentence overturned. After all, notorious Texas gunman John Wesley Hardin had also been tried for murder in 1877, but Hardin had been saved from the rope and given a twenty-five-year sentence at the state prison in Huntsville (*see Chapter Three*). If he did have faith in the legal process, it eventually diminished because in the spring of 1878 he attempted to escape. The *Victoria Advocate* reported: "He had procured a saw and had commenced operations when discovered. He writes a letter to the Civilian on the subject, saying that he will never 'Give away' the person who furnished him the implement, remarking that the jailor appeared 'to want a saw a darned sight worse than he did,' and that he unhesitatingly give it to him."[19]

On Wednesday, March 13, 1878, in a decision written by Judge John Preston White, the Court of Appeals ruled that there was insufficient evidence — there was no transcript — to rule for the defendant. The verdict and sentence stood. Bloody Bill Longley would hang on the gallows.

Aftermath

On August 24, 1878, Bill Longley was escorted by Sheriff James Madison Brown and several deputies by train from Galveston to Giddings. On September 6 he appeared again before Judge Turner, who set an execution date of October 11, between 11 a.m. and sunset. He continued to write friends and family. In a letter to a woman he had known since his school days, he included his famous quote: "Hanging is my favorite way of dying."

A *Galveston Daily News* reporter met with Longley in his cell on the day before the execution. "I found him calm, collected and in good spirits," the reporter wrote. "Though not as jocular as formerly, he has not gotten over his habit of speaking lightly of killing. In answer to the question if he had prepared any statement, he said 'No sir, I have none written, and don't think I will write any.' Answering the question, 'Will you make a speech?' said 'I don't know now. That depends upon how I feel at the time. I don't see what good it will do. Let others learn by experience as I have.' Longley appears heavier than ever known to be, and speaks most kindly of the treatment received in jail here, especially when comparing it with his incarceration in Galveston. The Catholic priest from Austin arrived this evening and spent some time with Longley. It is notable that Longley has left off using profane language entirely."[20]

Reporters were eventually barred from "annoying" the doomed man, who spent his last night with the Reverend Daniel J. Spillard, an Irish Catholic priest from Austin. At 8 a.m. Friday, October 11, Spillard and the French-born priest Joseph Querat met with Longley to perform the rite of extreme unction. "The morning...arose dark and lowering, a fit emblem of his fate," the *St. Louis Daily Globe-Democrat* reported. "As day broke, caravans of people — wagons, carriages, horsemen, women and men — lined the roads leading into the little town of Giddings, the scene of the hanging, all eager to catch a glimpse of the notorious desperado."[21]

After the priests finished the holy sacrament, Longley asked one of the guards to sing "Amazing Grace" and joined in on bass. After other songs, Longley put on a "faultless" black suit, white shirt, black necktie, turn down collar, and blue rosette on his coat lapel. Wearing a low-crown, broad-brimmed hat and with his hair, mustache, and goatee trimmed neatly, he "was probably one of the handsomest men present on the occasion."[22] His only visitor, according to the *Daily Globe-Democrat,* was his ten-year-old niece, Lizzie Karnes. He kissed her goodbye, and at 1:25 p.m., Sheriff James Madison Brown and four deputies escorted Longley to an ambulance. Newspaper accounts say Brown had deputized another one hundred guards, armed with shotguns and Winchesters, some mounted and the rest serving as "infantry." Guards and prisoner went down the street to the scaffold, reaching the execution site at 2 p.m.

Longley, with a cigar in his mouth, readily dismounted from the ambulance, walked between two guards to a seat, called for water, drank it, and spoke to several of his guards. At 2:15 the prisoner, with Fathers Spillard and Querat and the guards, ascended the scaffold by a stairway, which came near giving way. Longley said: "Look out, the steps are falling."[23]

The gallows held, however, and Sheriff Brown addressed the crowd gathered for the first legal hanging in Lee County, saying that he hoped there would never be cause for another such hanging. After the death warrant was read, Longley was asked if he had anything to say. According to the *Daily Globe-Democrat*, Longley took off his hat and spoke in a firm voice:

> I haven't much to say. I supposed I have to die. In the crowd before me I see the faces of many enemies, but few friends. I hope you will all forgive me, as I have forgiven you, and as God has forgiven me. I hear my brother is in the crowd, but I hope not. If any friends sympathize with me, I ask them not to attempt to take revenge in my behalf; I dread to die, but as it has to be I'll stand it; all men hate to die. I am all right, there is no one to blame but myself, and I hope my friends will not try to take revenge. I have killed men who hated to die as bad as I do.[24]

Longley knelt with the two priests to pray, after which his hands were shackled and he shook hands with everyone on the platform, even kissed the left cheek of Sheriff Brown. In a loud voice, he said, "Goodbye, all," and many spectators answered, "Goodbye, Bill." The trap door opened at 2:35 or 2:37 p.m.

"The body fell eight feet, as was intended. The rope slipped on the beam, and the body continued until the feet touched the earth, when sheriff Brown and an aid caught and raised it up and refastened it, leaving the body properly suspended. Two moans escaped the lips, and arms and feet were raised three times, and after hanging eleven and a half minutes life was pronounced extinct by Drs. Fields, Gasley and Johnson," the *Galveston Daily News* recorded. "When cut down the neck was found broken. The body was carted off and buried by sheriff Brown."[25]

The *Daily Globe-Democrat* noted that "Longley's last act before putting on the black cap was to wink at one of the guards and laugh outright." Another legend has it that after the body was cut down, Sheriff Brown took Longley's head in his hands and rotated it one hundred and eighty degrees.

Despite the eyewitness reports and large turnout for the execution (some say four thousand were on hand for the hanging), stories persisted that Bill Longley survived his execution. Longley lived out his days in Louisiana, or maybe South or Central America. He was a South American cattle baron who died when Germans torpedoed and sank the *Lusitania* in 1915. He changed his name to John Calhoun Brown, married, and lived a crime-free life in Louisiana until his death in 1921 in Iberville Parish. He cut a deal with Sheriff Brown to fake the execution. A bullet cut the rope. He wore a special harness that allowed him to survive his own hanging.

Legends can be hard to kill.

In the early 1990s, forensic scientists tried to find Longley's grave in Giddings and solve the mystery once and for all, but they couldn't locate the body. Forensic anthropologist Douglas Owsley didn't quit, however, and in 2001, the mystery was solved. The grave of the outlaw was found, complete with bones and the religious medal he had worn to the gallows. Using DNA testing that compared blood and saliva samples from Longley's great-great niece, Helen Chapman, with a tooth from the grave, scientists announced their findings on June 13, 2001, at the Smithsonian's National Museum of Natural History in Washington, D.C.

The man buried in Giddings was indeed William Preston Longley. Bloody Bill had not faked his execution. The man who said "hanging is my favorite way of dying" had indeed been hanged to death in Giddings, Texas, in 1878.

Chapter Notes

Primary sources: "Boastful Bill Longley: Cold-Blooded Texas Killer" (*Wild West*, February 2002) by Rick Miller; "Wild Bill Longley" (*Old West*, Winter 1965) by L. Patschke Rhodes; *Bloody Bill Longley* (Henington Publishing Company, 1996) by Rick Miller; *Triggernometry: A Gallery of Gunfighters* (University of Oklahoma Press, 1996) by Eugene Cunningham; and various editions of the 1877-78 *Galveston Daily News, St. Louis Daily Globe-Democrat, Dallas Daily Herald,* and *Victoria Advocate.*

1. *Galveston Daily News,* October 12, 1878.
2. Ibid.
3. Ibid.
4. *St. Louis Daily Globe-Democrat,* October 12, 1878.
5. Ibid.
6. *Galveston Daily News,* October 12, 1878.
7. Ibid.
8. *St. Louis Daily Globe-Democrat,* October 12, 1878.
9. *Galveston Daily News,* August 1, 1877.
10. *Galveston Daily News,* October 21, 1877.
11. Ibid.
12. *Galveston Daily News,* September 4, 1877.
13. *Galveston Daily News,* October 21, 1877.
14. *Galveston Daily News,* September 4, 1877.
15. *Galveston Daily News,* October 21, 1877.

16. Ibid.

17. *Dallas Daily Herald*, October 19, 1877.

18. *Victoria Advocate*, September 15, 1877.

19. *Victoria Advocate,* April 28, 1878.

20. *Galveston Daily News*, October 11, 1878.

21. *St. Louis Daily Globe-Democrat*, October 12, 1878.

22. Ibid.

23. *Galveston Daily News*, October 12, 1878.

24. *St. Louis Daily Globe-Democrat*, October 12, 1878.

25. *Galveston Daily News,* October 12, 1878.

"Live at peace with the white men"

Court-Martial of the Apache Scouts

<← — — — — — — — — — — — — — — — →>

Fort Grant, Arizona Territory, 1881

Prelude

He was called The Dreamer. An unassuming Cibecue Apache standing five-foot-six and weighing about one hundred and twenty-five pounds, if that, Nock-ay-det-klinne could have been in his mid-thirties or early fifties. Owensboro, Kentucky-born Thomas Cruse, a twenty-three-year-old lieutenant in the Sixth Cavalry, described him this way: "His face — very light in color for an Apache — was drawn and ascetic-looking. It was an interesting face in every way."[1] Yet as a medicine man, Nock-ay-det-klinne held much influence with his people, treating and counseling the Apaches as any good medicine man would. In 1871 he had apparently been chosen to go to Washington, D.C., with a delegation of Apaches to meet President Ulysses S. Grant (records don't list his name, but that doesn't mean he wasn't there) and returned with a presidential medal and stories of white power. Cruse suggests that The Dreamer also learned the white man's religion at a school in Santa Fe, New Mexico, and became fascinated with the tale of

Christ's resurrection. Ten years later he was preaching to his people, but it wasn't exactly the gospel taught in Sunday school.

In fact, it was scaring the hell out of white authorities around the White Mountain Indian Reservation in eastern Arizona.

Upon receiving permission from the Indian agent, Nock-ay-det-klinne moved his small band to Cibecue Creek, some forty-five miles northwest of Fort Apache, in May 1881. A month later authorities were receiving word that The Dreamer had been holding some type of "revival meetings" in which the Apaches drank *tizwin*, a weak Apache beer made from mescal or corn, and danced with enthusiasm until they passed out from exhaustion. The dancing, drinking, and

A view of an Apache camp on the San Carlos River in the 1880s.
(Courtesy, Denver Public Library, Western History Department)

singing didn't really scare soldiers, but The Dreamer's message certainly worried them.

Nock-ay-det-klinne said the dances would help raise two Apache chiefs from the dead and, some said, make the whites vanish from Apache country. Nine years later a similar prophecy would lead to the bloody Sioux-Seventh Cavalry clash at Wounded Knee in present-day South Dakota. The Sioux "ghost dance" — Cruse notes that the term wasn't in vogue in 1881 — remains one of the most heartbreaking events of the Indian Wars, but what happened at Cibecue Creek, Arizona, in 1881 is equally tragic. Neither Wounded Knee nor Cibecue Creek should have happened, and both can be blamed on an overzealous army and poor judgment on each side.

On June 18 Sixth Cavalry commander Colonel Eugene Asa Carr arrived at Fort Apache. A career soldier known as "War Eagle," Carr was born in Erie County, New York, on March 10, 1830, and graduated from the U.S. Military Academy at West Point in 1850 with a dismal 212 conduct standing in a corps of 220. He served in the Mounted Rifles and First Cavalry in Texas, Kansas, and Indian Territory before the Civil War, then fought for the Union, taking three wounds and earning the Medal of Honor for his bravery at Pea Ridge, Arkansas, in 1862. By the end of the war, Carr had been breveted a major general.

After the war Carr received a major's commission in the Fifth Cavalry. He saw action against Indians in Kansas and Colorado in 1868-69, including the historic Battle at Summit Springs. During the Indian campaigns of 1876, Carr also took part in the fight against the Cheyennes at War Bonnet Creek, Wyoming, with Colonel Wesley Merritt and William F. "Buffalo Bill" Cody, the latter a scout who had distinguished himself with Carr at Summit Springs. Later Carr engaged the Sioux at

Called "War Eagle," Sixth Cavalry Colonel Eugene Asa Carr was in command at Fort Apache during the Cibecue uprising. (National Archives)

Slim Buttes in Dakota Territory. By the time he was promoted to colonel and assumed command of the Sixth Cavalry in 1879, Carr was a battle-savvy Indian fighter.

Almost immediately upon his arrival at Fort Apache, Colonel Carr heard from the San Carlos Indian agent, Joseph Capron Tiffany, a fat lout whom the Apaches called "Big Belly." Tiffany had been appointed agent in March 1880 and reached San Carlos on June 1.

Tiffany, 52, had done just about everything before becoming an Indian agent. Reared in Baltimore, Maryland, Tiffany had worked in farm fields and businesses in New York, tried his hand at lumbering in Virginia, experimented in the commercial ice business in Maine, and, after serving in the Union army during the Civil War — Lieutenant Cruse referred to him as Major Tiffany — planted cotton and tobacco in Virginia. His tenure as district judge and help with the newly freed slaves in Virginia, coupled with his work in the Methodist Episcopal Church and temperance leanings, led to his appointment at San Carlos.

By the first of 1881, Tiffany had transitioned easily into his new job. In fact, historian John Bret Harte noted in the *Journal of Arizona History*, that Tiffany's "administration was smoother and generally more successful than that of any previous agent except John Philip Crum."[2] He had opened an Indian school and began construction on an irrigation system. After coal was discovered near the agency in early 1881, however, Tiffany's smooth transition ended. The agent angered settlers when he refused to return the coal beds to public domain and advised Apache leaders to lease the mineral rights, a plan the Department of the Interior refused to authorize, and soon he became linked to what soldier and chronicler John G. Bourke called the "infamous Tucson ring," a greedy lot interested in stealing coal for profit and other methods of graft. Charges of fraud, speculation, conspiracy, larceny and, most importantly, the mistreatment of Apache prisoners would bring about Tiffany's downfall. Nock-ay-det-klinne and the Cibecue affair would not help matters, either.

The Dreamer's original vision was one of peace, simply the revival of two dead Apache chiefs. After long dancing and still no sign of the dead chiefs, Nock-ay-det-klinne proclaimed that the spirits had spoken to him again, informing him "that the dead warriors could not return to the country until the whites had left it...."[3] Charles Collins, perhaps the most noted chronicler of the Cibecue outbreak and aftermath, writes in *The Great Escape: The Apache Outbreak of 1881*: "Probably, [Nock-ay-det-klinne] was not seriously advocating the departure of the whites, but was trying to save face and his own life by tying the resurrections to an unlikely event."[4]

In any event, once the Apaches began dreaming of a land without whites, Agent Tiffany, the settlers, and the army grew concerned.

In August, Lieutenant Cruse, in charge of the Indian scout company at Fort Apache, ordered his chief of scouts to ride over to Carrizo Creek, watch the dances, and report back. Sam Bowman, who has been identified as either a Cherokee or Choctaw, returned and tendered his resignation. Cruse asked for an explanation, but Bowman would say only that he had been in the territory for seven years and wanted to go back to Indian Territory (present-day Oklahoma). Cruse reluctantly accepted the resignation, and Sam Bowman lit a shuck out of Arizona. Cruse never associated the scout's resignation with the Apache dancing until he asked chief packer Nat Nobles about it. Nobles explained that Bowman "said that kind of dance always meant trouble with his people. He believed that it would bring the same here and he didn't want to get mixed up in it. So he decided to go see his folks."[5]

The first hint of trouble among Cruse's Apache scouts came when he gave some passes to attend the dancing — after all, it was part of their culture — and they returned in bad moods, irritated at white expansion into what once was Apache land. Some became insubordinate, which surprised the young lieutenant because the scouts had always been loyal. Meanwhile at the San Carlos Agency, Tiffany was having trouble as well. The agent had requested that Nock-ay-det-klinne come to the agency to talk and to hold his dances at San Carlos (most likely so white authorities could keep a closer eye on the goings-on), but The Dreamer said no. Tiffany sent his Indian police to bring in the medicine man, but The Dreamer's followers disarmed the policemen.

On a mesa overlooking Cibecue during dancing/fasting, The Dreamer's followers said three dead leaders rose. Years after the incident, an Apache told Cruse:

> They were like shadows at first, but we saw them rise out of the ground, very slowly, and coming no farther than the knees. All about them they looked, then to us they said:
>
> "Why do you call upon us? Why do you disturb us? We do not wish to come back. The buffalo are gone. White people are everywhere in the land that was ours. We do not wish to come back."
>
> And we cried to them, saying:
>
> "But tell us what we must do!"
>
> And they answered us as they began to sink into the ground and to become as shadows:
>
> "Live at peace with the white men and let us rest."[6]

To some Apaches, the appearance and words of the three dead chiefs proclaimed that, yes, there was life after death, but many warriors cried out that it meant they should wipe out the whites. Surprisingly, despite the final command to "Live at peace with the white men," only a few interpreted the vision as a call for peace.

As the situation grew more and more tense, Tiffany called on the army to help. Hearing reports that the Apache scouts were growing disloyal, Colonel Carr on August 10 asked Cruse for suggestions, and the lieutenant offered that he take his company to Fort Huachuca, in the Tombstone area, and have his company be replaced by Huachuca's company of Mojave and Yuma scouts. Private George Hurle, who spoke Apache, reiterated Cruse's plan, and three days later Carr telegraphed General Orlando B. Willcox, commander of the Department of Arizona, requesting the transfer. Willcox approved the plan, but the telegraph lines went down and, in a twist of tragic fate, Carr did not receive the wire until two and a half weeks later.

On August 14 Carr ordered Cruse to disarm his Apache scouts after inspection. The lieutenant told the Apaches the guns would be kept in an office to protect them from the rain, and although the scouts didn't like this — rightfully considering it a sign of distrust — they went along with it.

The telegraph line was repaired on August 28, and Carr received an order from General Willcox. At four o'clock that afternoon, Officers' Call sounded, and Cruse and other officers reported to Carr, who read the order and then passed the paper around for all to see. Willcox had sided with Tiffany and told Carr to kill or capture Nock-ay-det-klinne. Carr then asked Cruse if they should take the Apache scouts with them on the assignment, and the lieutenant replied it would be better to have the scouts with them.

As he explained later: "I understood the circumstances, thought it far more dangerous to leave them behind at Fort Apache, which was left garrisoned by only thirty men, than to take them along with us."[7]

Carr agreed, and the following morning the colonel left Fort Apache to bring in The Dreamer. With him were seventy-nine enlisted men from D and E Troops, twenty-three Indian scouts, and five officers. One of the officers was Captain Edmund C. Hentig, who was waiting to return to Philadelphia on recruiting duty and to visit his wife, sick in a hospital.

Cruse and the Apache scouts reached Cibecue on the afternoon of August 30, where they were greeted by several Apaches, carrying weapons and wearing war paint. One of them called Cruse by his not-so-nice Apache nickname, *Nantan Eclatten*, or "Raw Virgin Lieutenant." The rest of the troop arrived later, and, through an interpreter, Carr began addressing Nock-ay-det-klinne, who was stretched out underneath his brush arbor after a long night of dancing. Carr told The Dreamer that he needed to come to the post and reassured him that no harm would come to him unless the Apaches resisted.

"Say that I cannot go now," Nock-ay-det-klinne answered. "I have matters of importance to settle before leaving this place. Say that if the soldiers will go back to their post I will follow soon — within three or four days."

Shaking his head, Carr shot back: "No! That won't do! Tell him he must come with me now!"

Followers of The Dreamer became agitated, and soldiers grew nervous, but an Apache scout called Sergeant Mose told

Nock-ay-det-klinne, in a voice loud enough for all to hear, that he would not be harmed. Everyone relaxed.

Carr ordered Sergeant John McDonald to take Nock-ay-det-klinne prisoner, warning him: "You will permit nobody to harm him. But if he attempts to escape, or if any of his people try to rescue him, shoot him instantly." McDonald and Mose led Nock-ay-det-klinne away; The Dreamer did not resist.

The Sixth Cavalry soldiers, Apache scouts, and prisoner left without incident, although several Apaches paralleled Carr's command to make sure nothing happened to Nock-ay-det-klinne. A short while later the soldiers began making camp, but when several Apaches started crossing Cibecue Creek just below the army position, Carr shouted: "Here! Those Indians mustn't come into camp! Direct the troop commanders to keep them out!"

Apaches later said all they wanted to do was watch and prevent any harm from coming to Nock-ay-det-klinne. His pistol holstered in his saddle, Captain Hentig began approaching the warriors, telling them: *"Ukashe! Ukashe!* (Get away! Get away!)"[8] Dandy Jim, an Apache scout, identified himself and kept walking toward Hentig, and the captain let him stand at his side.

Tension mounted, and suddenly gunfire erupted.

Dandy Jim, according to white witnesses, shot down Hentig, while other Apaches opened fire on Hentig's orderly, Private Edward Livingstone, killing him. Following orders, Sergeant McDonald shot Nock-ay-det-klinne and almost immediately was felled by a bullet in his leg. Wounded, Nock-ay-det-klinne tried to crawl away, but D Troop trumpeter William Benites saw him, put his pistol against the medicine man's head, and pulled the trigger. A civilian guide then split The Dreamer's forehead with an axe. That's the white version of the attack. Apaches claimed that Nock-ay-det-klinne was shot before the Indians opened fire.

Nock-ay-det-klinne's wife and son also died during the attack. The son charged on his father's horse and was killed. Seeing her son fall, Nock-ay-det-klinne's wife picked up Hentig's pistol, pointed it at a soldier, and was shot down.

The soldiers drove off the Apaches, including several mutinous or just plain frightened scouts. Cruse estimated some eight hundred Apaches had gathered around the Cibecue by sunset. In addition to Hentig and Livingstone, Carr had lost five other soldiers, not to mention fifty-five horses and mules. He did not include six dead scouts, considered turncoats. The other dead soldiers were privates William Miller, Henry C. Bird, John Sondregger, John Sullivan, and Thomas J. Foran, all of D Troop. Sondregger and Bird lived till about sundown, and Foran died just after sunrise as Carr limped back to Fort Apache.

On September 1 the Apaches attacked Fort Apache — a scene used frequently in Western movies but seldom witnessed on the frontier — but were repulsed, and the warring Indians and deserting scouts went into hiding. Rumors swept through the country that Carr's command had been wiped out. Cruse would later read his own obituary, and *The New York Times* would run a headline claiming "Gen. Carr and His Command Murdered," but the colonel noted in a dispatch published in the *Chicago Times*: "While lamenting the death by treachery of Capt. Hentig and the men who fell with him, I am rejoiced to report that the massacre of Carr's command is not true."[9]

General George Crook replaced Willcox as commander of the Department of Arizona on September 4, 1882, and peace eventually returned to Arizona Territory. By early October sixty hostiles had surrendered, including several scouts, who would soon learn about white man's justice.

Because they were enlisted soldiers, Sergeant Dandy Jim, Sergeant Dead Shot, and Corporal Skippy, plus a Private Mucheco, were to be tried by military court-martial, which convened in November 1881 at Fort Grant.

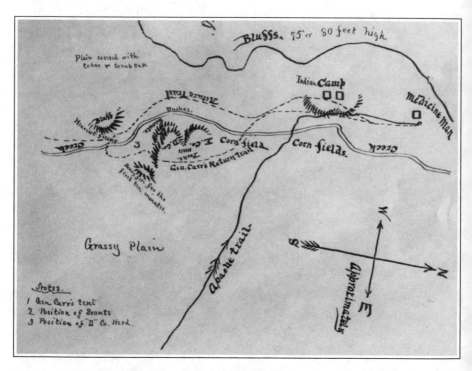

Lieutenant Thomas Cruse's sketch of the Cibecue Creek fight appeared with his court-martial testimony. (National Archives)

Trial

The charges facing Dandy Jim, Dead Shot, and Skippy were:

I. Violation of the 21st Article of War: Offering violence against superior officers by raising a gun against them and shooting at them and the troops under their command.

II. Mutiny, in violation of the 22nd Article of War, for resisting and firing upon the forces of the United States.

III. Violation of the 23rd Article of War, for being present at and having knowledge of a mutiny against the commanding officer and failing to use utmost endeavors to suppress the same or to give information thereof to the commanding officer.

IV. Desertion, in violation of the 47th Article of War.

V. Murder, in violation of the 58th Article of War.

On November 11, 1881, nine officers of the Sixth Cavalry and Eighth and Twelfth Infantry convened at Fort Grant for the trial of Sergeant No. 4, alias Dead Shot. Captain Harry Clay Egbert, Twelfth Infantry, was appointed judge advocate, and Major James Biddle, Sixth Cavalry, was court president. Under military regulations, a court-martial panel needed no fewer than five and no more than thirteen officers.

Two interpreters, Charles (or, perhaps, George) Hurle and Merdifilda Grijalba, were sworn in, and Second Lieutenant Elon Farnsworth Willcox, Twelfth Infantry, was approved as defense counsel. Willcox was former department commander Orlando Willcox's son, had been out of the United States Military Academy only three years, and had no legal experience. Yet he immediately requested a "ban of trial" on the murder charge and specification. His argument:

> The 58th Article of War as far as courts martial are concerned is only triable in time of war and at other

times only by civil courts of criminal jurisdiction. To my best knowledge and judgment the United States declines to recognize hostilities with Indians as a state of war. The Indian is not a citizen of the United States, therefore it cannot be civil war. They are not recognized as a sovereign power, therefore it is not international or foreign war. These are the two classes into which war is divided. The Indian is simply a ward of the nation and as such the nation punishes him for his misdeeds but this is not war.[10]

Judge Advocate Egbert argued otherwise and pointed to the military commission at Fort Klamath, Oregon, in 1873, that resulted in the conviction and execution of the Modocs (*See Chapter One*). Willcox fired back:

The case of the Modocs stands probably alone in the history of the country. The murder was committed under a flag of truce borne by the United States. The mere fact of presenting a flag of truce to these Indians admitted a state of war which the United States was bound to sustain by trial by military commission. This is not a parallel case and I doubt very much if in Washington a state of war will be admitted.

After a closed session, the court ruled against the defense petition, and Dead Shot entered a plea of not guilty to all charges and specifications. The first witness called by the judge advocate was Lieutenant Cruse.

Questioned by Egbert, Cruse testified that he had known Dead Shot for eighteen months, and that the Apache had served in the company of scouts several times. Enlistments

Dandy Jim, a sergeant, was one of the Apache scouts put on trial for the Cibecue mutiny in the military court-martial at Fort Grant. (Courtesy, Arizona Historical Society/Tucson. Negative Number 41254)

were for six months, and Dead Shot had last enlisted on June 6, 1881. The questioning went on:

Q: Does a scout sign any papers of enlistment?

A: They do, by mark.

Q: What is the mode of enlistment?

A: Notice is given two or three days previous to time of enlistment that a new company is to be enlisted and all the Indians who wish to enlist are present on that day. They form in line and I pick out the twenty-five men whom I wish for scouts. They are then given belts with tags and made non-commissioned officers according to their numbers. As soon as practicable regular enlistment papers are made out signed by the recruiting officer of the post and signed by mark by the Indian and they are then notified that they are soldiers in the United States service.

Egbert continued on this line of interrogation, noting that the scouts were paid for their services, and then brought the witness to the matter of the Cibecue Creek fight.

Cruse testified that Colonel Carr had just given him orders as to where he should hold Nock-ay-det-klinne when he heard a war whoop and a soldier shout: "Watch out, they are going to shoot." Before Cruse could turn, gunfire erupted and he dropped to the ground, leaving Nock-ay-det-klinne and several members of his company.

"Did you see the parties firing, I mean as a body?" the judge advocate asked.

"I did."

"Who were they?"

"They were my scouts."

Lieutenant William Stanton then took his company to force back the Indians, while others dug in for defense, Cruse said, adding that Stanton's command drove the scouts into the bushes and finally across Cibecue Creek.

Cruse's testimony continued when the court-martial resumed on November 12. He said Dead Shot did not rejoin the company, and he put him down as deserted on the rolls until informed of the scout's capture. He recalled his conversation with Colonel Carr of August 10 about the loyalty of the scouts and mentioned that many were angry on the way to Cibecue Creek because they recommended one trail, but the troops chose another.

"Which trail would be most favorable to ambushes?" Egbert asked.

Cruse answered: "The one they wanted us to take."

Under cross-examination by Willcox, Cruse said he did not see Dead Shot after or during the first volley and, in fact, never saw him fire his weapon. Willcox then asked if the enlistment papers had been read and explained to the scouts. Cruse said they had not because he had been told the oath could not be adequately translated into Apache.

Q: Did you ever read the Articles of War to the prisoner? Did he know of their existence? Did he understand fully the liabilities and responsibilities he assumed by his enlistment?

A: I never read the Articles of War to the prisoner, but I think the scouts had a very clear idea of the obedience they owed to their superiors officers and to the general government. No translation has ever been made of the Articles of War into their language.

Q: You say you *think* they had a very clear idea of their duties, can you not be more explicit?

A: I know it was well understood among them that if they did not do what they were told they would be punished and that they owed obedience to the officers that the Indians who had not been enlisted did not owe.

Still questioned by the court, Cruse talked about Carr's order to disarm the scouts and then was asked if he could have held the scouts in the post guardhouse.

"If I had been ordered to do so, I think I could have done so," he said.

"If you had disarmed them and confined them, would they have been dangerous in the post?"

"I don't think they would."

Next up for the prosecution was First Lieutenant William Harding Carter, the Sixth Cavalry's regimental quartermaster, who was at the Cibecue battle as acting adjutant of two companies. In 1891 Carter and two other soldiers would be awarded the Medal of Honor for pulling the wounded from fire. He gave a detailed but quite mundane account of the events leading up to the fight. After hearing the Apache war whoop, however, he testified:

I called towards Captain Hentig in a loud tone of voice to look out, one of two shots were immediately fired from among the strange Indians and then a scattering fire took place from among the strange Indians. I turned towards the scouts, who were just at my right hand, a few feet off, to see what they were going to do. I looked at Dead Shot, who was in charge of them, as I thought his action would probably indicate what the rest of them would probably do. He said something to them in Indian and he and all the rest whom I could see raised their guns and fired in the direction of Captain Hentig and his troops. I then drew my revolver and fired at Dandy Bill, a sergeant of the scouts, who was nearest to me — about twelve or fifteen feet off — I saw that I was alone and endeavored to get behind the corner of the tent, which was still five or six yards from me. The sergeant major, who was lying in the grass near me, called for me to drop. I turned around and faced the scouts just as a number of them raised their guns. I dropped on the grass. The volley was fired by them and went over me. By this time a fire commenced from the soldiers in various parts of the camp and the scouts began to break and run down the mesa into the brush.

He also pointed out that the scouts were armed with .45-caliber Springfield breech-loading rifles.

"How many times did you see the prisoner, Dead Shot, fire?" the judge advocate asked.

"I only saw him fire at the first volley that the scouts fired, but I should judge by the number of bullets that went over me as I lay down that all of them must have fired. I mean the second volley."

"Did you notice him aiming at any one?"

"No sir. I simply saw him aiming in the direction of the company. I had the men killed and wounded brought in and most of them fell in the place towards which the first volley was directed. Private Livingstone, Captain Hentig's orderly, was standing immediately in front of where the scouts fired and only a few feet off. He had three balls in him and was undoubtedly killed by the first volley."

Under cross-examination, Carter said he could not say for certain that Dead Shot killed Captain Hentig, but added: "I think he was instrumental in his death: that if he had used his influence with the scouts the greater part of them would have stayed with us."

Carter also testified that he did not see Dead Shot fire or raise his gun at any officer, but when asked for a clarification by the judge advocate, he explained that he did not witness Dead Shot aiming at any officer "specially," but rather only saw him aiming in the direction of Hentig and D Troop.

He went on to testify that he thought most of the soldiers killed had been shot by mutinous scouts and "strange Indians."

The next witness called was Assistant Surgeon George McCreery, first lieutenant and post surgeon at Fort Apache. McCreery had given the scouts a physical during their June enlistment and was at the Cibecue fight, but most of his testimony concerned the wounded and dead. All wounds were caused by .45-caliber gunshots, McCreery said. He could distinguish between calibers this way: "The wound inflicted by a 45 caliber would admit the little finger with a little pressing — with the 50 you could admit it much more readily. A 45 caliber wound through bone would not admit the little finger."

Willcox, once again, kept his cross-examination short, relying on the surgeon's testimony that he had not seen Dead Shot fire at anyone.

Next up for the prosecution were civilian scouts. John Byrne, chief of scouts, and John L. Colvig recalled the fight. Willcox didn't bother questioning Byrne but had to cross-examine Colvig after he testified that he recognized Dead Shot, although he was seventy yards away, firing at the troops.

"Are you *positive* you saw Dead Shot fire; could you not have mistaken another Indian for him?" Willcox asked.

"No sir," Colvig answered. "I am positive of that fact."

That was his only question, although the court asked if Colvig knew if Dead Shot was a good marksman. Colvig did not know.

After more repetitive testimony from D Troop Privates John Burton and Ludwig Baege, neither of whom were cross-examined by Willcox, farrier Eugene Condon of D Troop recalled the arrival of Dandy Jim, the Apaches, and Captain Hentig trying to make them leave the camp. "One Indian, Dandy Jim, one of the scouts dismounted and came around between Captain Hentig and the Indian on the horse. Captain Hentig caught Jim by the shoulder and told him to [*Ukashe*], not knowing that he was a soldier. He replied 'I am a soldier.' Captain said, 'Well, if you're a soldier go to camp,' and pushed him around to the left of himself. Jim went around behind him looking sideways at him as he went along and when he got a few feet behind him, he knelt down and fired right towards him. Captain Hentig threw up his hands and said, 'Oh! My God' and fell."

Questioned by Willcox, the farrier said he did not know if Dandy Jim fired the first shot or had killed Hentig, nor did he see Dead Shot during the fight.

Other witnesses, including Sergeants John McDonald and John H. Smith, were questioned by the judge advocate but not the defense counsel. Smith said he saw Dead Shot fire at Private Livingstone, who fell dead instantly, and then the scout dropped his gun and ran out of the camp. Sergeant Daniel Conn also swore to seeing Dead Shot fire at Livingstone. The parade of witnesses for the prosecution continued, with most of them repeating testimony. The last witness was Agent

Joseph C. Tiffany, who said Dead Shot arrived at the agency in October and told him he was a scout. The agent had his policemen arrest him and turn him over to Lieutenant Colonel William Redwood Price of the Sixth Cavalry.

For defense witnesses, Willcox recalled Assistant Surgeon McCreery and Lieutenant Carter, prompting them to testify that Private Livingstone had received multiple gunshot wounds. Then, through the interpreters, Dead Shot gave the court his version of the Cibecue fight:

Then the Cibecue Indians came in. They appeared to be quarrelsome. Mose called me and told me to take his (Mose's) stepson's horse and follow General Carr. I did so and overtook General Carr before he got into camp and told him that both the Indians and the American soldiers appeared to be quarrelsome. General Carr told me that was all right that he did not think it would amount to anything. I then turned back and recrossed the river. I rejoined the Indian company which was already moving down on the other side of the river with the medicine man. The boy who had loaned me the horse told me he wanted it back. I returned it to him and went along with the other Indians on foot. As we went along I noticed Mose having hold of the medicine man. The Cibecue Indians kept coming in and I told them to go away. They were mad with me and began to strip themselves as they went along. As we came close to the American camp as we rode up the mesa there were about seven of us scouts together. The rest of the scouts were coming in twos and threes. I told him to close up not to be straggling around like that. We — the scouts — were going toward General Carr's tent when we met Lieutenant

Carter, who showed us a place to camp. There were ants there and I told him that was not a good place to sleep. So Lieutenant Carter told me to come over farther from the ants and camp there. I started some of the scouts after our mess box for we were hungry by that time. I leaned my gun against a soapweed and started to go and get wood when I heard two shots. When I heard the first two shots, I thought someone was shooting at some duck in the creek and then I heard four shots fired and then I saw the Indian soldiers whom I had left behind me when I went for wood break and run in the brush. I then asked them what was the matter. They told me the Americans and Indians were fighting one another. I ran to get my gun when I saw myself alone and the Americans were charging towards me. I have ten fingers and two eyes and the Americans accuse me of killing which I did not do. I never put my finger on the trigger of my gun. This much is true. I ran on the other side of the creek. If the scouts had anyone to talk to them they would not have run away as they did. No one gave them any orders. No one told them what to do. I make this statement because I never did any shooting. I was always known to tell the truth. I never tell a lie. I have been a soldier since I was young. I was always well treated; always got sugar, coffee and all such necessaries by being a soldier and I had no notion of quitting soldiering. When my time expired I intended to enlist again. I am now accused of shooting and probably the court will believe I did shoot. I did not. If I had shot I would not have come in . . . .

The trial of Dandy Jim, Sergeant No. 4, convened on November 16 with the same court personnel. Thomas Cruse again was the prosecution's first witness, and witnesses and testimony proceeded along the same lines as during Dead Shot's trial. In his statement, Dandy Jim said that he was not in the direction of Hentig when the captain approached the arriving Apaches. "I heard two shots fired and after the whole volley," the scout said. "When I heard them I put my gun on my shoulder and went down into the hollow by myself. That night I camped alone."

Dandy Jim went on to say: "The Americans have their habits and the Indian has his. All the scouts here that gave themselves up were not hostile. If they had been they would not have done so. The witnesses against me differ. Some say I rode into camp. Some say that I walked in. They differ. I do not."

Skippy's trial began on November 16 and again proceeded with the same personnel and many of the same questions and answers, but Skippy was a little different from Dead Shot and Dandy Jim. In his report to Secretary of War Robert Lincoln, the judge advocate general in Washington pointed out: "Skippy is represented as a silly kind of Indian singing and dancing and 'poking fun' at other Indians, but is a reliable scout and appears to be responsible for his acts and conduct."[11]

Captain William Scott Worth of the Eighth Infantry was even called as a defense witness and talked about Skippy's nature. "He was always considered a good natured, trifling sort of Indian and always fond of singing." When Willcox asked if Skippy would have been singing and dancing while intending to fight soldiers and commit mutiny, however, Worth gave an answer that certainly pleased Egbert. "I think he would," Worth said. "He is a silly kind of an Indian and would be as likely to be singing and dancing then as at any other time."

In his statement, Skippy said he was sick at the time of the Cibecue affair. After the capture of The Dreamer, Skippy had laid down on a knoll to rest. He was on his way to the army camp when he heard shooting. He heard the Cibecue Apaches yelling to shoot, and he turned back and went to another Indian camp, which he found deserted. He finally returned to Carrizo looking for his wife but could not find her.

"I then started for the Sub Agency and was delayed at the Salt River three days on account of high water," he said. "After I got to the Gila I was called by an Indian who told me my wife was at the Sub Agency sick. The next day I swam the river which was very high." At the subagency, Skippy turned in his weapon, plus twenty rounds of ammunition, and was taken to Fort Thomas and put in the guardhouse. "Then I was told it was all right and that I could enlist again which I did and became a soldier," he concluded.

In the end, Skippy, Dead Shot, and Dandy Jim were convicted on all charges and specifications and were sentenced to death. Private No. 15, Mucheco, was convicted of "joining in a mutiny and having knowledge of an intended mutiny, failing to give information thereof, and of desertion," and was sentenced to life imprisonment at Alcatraz Prison in San Francisco. Another private, No. 11, was later tried and sentenced to eight years at Alcatraz.

The judge advocate general approved the findings, as did President Chester A. Arthur. The execution was set for March 3, 1882.

Aftermath

The three condemned men were shackled and confined in separate cells. Three weeks before the execution date, however, Dandy Jim somehow freed himself from his irons and made a dash for freedom. He ran about five hundred yards before a guard fired, wounding him in his left arm. A few days before his execution, Dandy Jim signaled for a woman walking to the post sutler's store to come by the window in the guardhouse. He gave her a necklace made of red glass and turquoise and told her, "You take, me pretty soon hang."

On March 3 a crowd of about two hundred, most of them soldiers, gathered around the gallows. The *Arizona Daily Star* reported that the prisoners:

> . . . ate sparingly of the breakfast placed before them this morning and did not once look in the direction of the gallows. After breakfast, Skippy asked how many hours he had to live, and when told it made a marked effect on his appearance.[12]

Handcuffed, the prisoners returned to their cells until 12:20 p.m., when they were escorted twenty yards to the gallows and climbed the steps. The *Daily Star* reported:

> Their hands and feet were then securely pinioned and they were told that if they had anything to say sufficient time would be allowed. All gave much the same answer — that it was not right to hang them. The white men had given them good clothes and food, but were now going to take all away from them. They were satisfied to die, as they would meet all their friends gone before them. Dead Shot said that he had suffered a good deal in this world and would be soon

at rest and felt happy. The chaplain then offered up prayers for their souls, and at three minutes past 1 the black caps were drawn over their heads, the noose examined and at five minutes past one the lever which supported the trap was pulled and the three men were launched into eternity. There was no perceptible struggle, only with Dandy Jim, over whose body a slight tremor passed for a couple of seconds."[13]

Dandy Jim, Skippy, and Dead Shot were buried near the post. Dead Shot was probably about forty years old. Skippy and Dandy Jim were not older than twenty-one.

The two privates sentenced to Alcatraz were paroled on June 29, 1884. Joseph Tiffany's reign as Indian agent would end in scandal. In the fall of 1882, a federal grand jury handed down thirty indictments against him, and the *Daily Star* called him and his ring "a disgrace to the civilization of the age, and a foul blot upon the national escutcheon."[14] Tiffany, sick and in financial woes, had left the agency in April 1882 and resigned on June 30. The charges would later be dropped because of a weak case made even weaker by the disappearance of a key prosecution witness. Tiffany took up cattle ranching in New Mexico and died in 1889.

Elon Willcox had an uneventful military career, and his biggest assignment might have been his duty as acting superintendent of Yosemite National Park in California for almost three months in 1899. Harry Egbert, on the other hand, rose to the rank of lieutenant colonel and was killed in action in the Philippines during the Spanish-American War.

Eugene Asa Carr survived a clash with General Willcox, who indicted him for mishandling the Cibecue incident, but Carr was exonerated by a court of inquiry and continued to serve with distinction in the army. He was promoted to brigadier general in 1892, and forced to retire the following year. He retired to Washington, D.C., and died in 1910. He was buried with full military honors at West Point.

Thomas Cruse also continued to serve in the army. He won the Medal of Honor for his actions at Big Dry Fork, Arizona, on July 17, 1882, after he "gallantly charged hostile Indians, and with his carbine compelled a party of them to keep under cover of their breastworks, thus being enabled to recover a wounded soldier." The award was issued ten years after the battle. Cruse was a brigadier general when he retired to Longport, New Jersey, in 1918. He died on June 8, 1943, and was buried in Arlington National Cemetery.

The Cibecue affair would eventually be overshadowed by other Apache outbreaks. Geronimo would gain plenty of national attention in the 1880s, while Dead Shot, Dandy Jim, and Skippy, not to mention Nock-ay-det-klinne, would be largely forgotten. So would Dead Shot's wife.

On March 3, 1882, the same day Dead Shot and his colleagues were hanged, Dead Shot's wife committed suicide by hanging herself from a tree at San Carlos, sixty miles from Fort Grant. The Apaches said she loved her husband so much, she was willing to go with him into eternity, even with a broken neck.

Chapter Notes

Primary sources: "Aftermath of Cibecue, Court Martial of the Apache Scouts, 1881," *The Smoke Signal* (Fall 1978) by Sidney B. Brinckerhoff; *On the Border with Crook* (Charles Scribner's Sons, 1891) by John G. Bourke; *Apache Nightmare: The Battle at Cibecue Creek* (University of Oklahoma Press, 1999) and *The Great Escape:*

The Apache Outbreak of 1881 (Westernlore Press, 1994), both by Charles Collins; *Apache Days and After* (University of Nebraska Press, 1987) by Thomas Cruse; "The Strange Case of Joseph C. Tiffany: Indian Agent in Disgrace" (*Journal of Arizona History*, Winter 1975) by John Bret Harte; *Fighting Men of the Indian Wars* (Barbed Wire Press, 1991) by Bill O'Neal; *Once They Moved Like the Wind: Cochise, Geronimo, and the Apache Wars* (Simon & Schuster, 1993) by David Roberts; "Apache Ghost Dance" (*Wild West*, August 1995) by Don Worcester; Annual Report of the Commissioner of Indian Affairs to the Secretary of the Department of Interior for the Year 1881, Report of the Commissioner of Indian Affairs, October 24, 1881; Records of the Judge Advocate General's Office, RG 153, Court-Martial Case Files, Trial of Enlisted Men at Fort Grant, Arizona Territory, 1881; *Chicago Times*, Sept. 6, 1881; and *Arizona Daily Star*, March 4 and October 24, 1882.

1. Cruse, *Apache Days and After*, pp. 93-94, 105-106.

2. Harte, John Bret, "The Strange Case of Joseph C. Tiffany: Indian Agent in Disgrace," *Journal of Arizona History*, No. 16, Vol. 4, Winter 1975, p. 386.

3. Annual Report of the Commissioner of Indian Affairs to the Secretary of the Department of Interior for the Year 1881, Report of the Commissioner of Indian Affairs, October 24, 1881.

4. Collins, Charles, *The Great Escape*, p. 1.

5. Cruse, p. 95.

6. Cruse, p. 98.

7. Records of the Judge Advocate General's Office, RG 153, Court-Martial Case Files, Trial of Enlisted Men at Fort Grant, Arizona Territory, 1881, hereafter referred to as Court-Martial Records.

8. Dialogue from Cruse, pp. 106-111.

9. *Chicago Times*, Sept. 6, 1881.

10. Court-martial records. Unless otherwise noted, all quoted material regarding the trial comes from the transcripts.

11. Ibid.

12. *Arizona Daily Star*, March 4, 1882.

13. Ibid.

14. *Arizona Daily Star*, October 24, 1882.

Chapter Six

"HUMAN JERKED BEEF"

Trial of Alfred Packer

Lake City, Colorado, 1883

Prelude

The story of Alfred G. Packer remains one of the American West's greatest unsolved mysteries — and a gruesome one at that. Heck, historians still debate his first name. Most records use the common spelling, but Packer often signed his name "Alferd," and some newspapers reported that he even had a tattoo on his right arm reading:

Alferd Packer
Camp Thomason
Second Battalion
16th Infantry

Alfred or Alferd, the slender, five-foot-ten-and-a-half Pennsylvanian with long chestnut hair and blue eyes, who spoke in an irritating, whiny, high-pitched voice, would become the main course of the most sensational murder case ever to titillate yet turn the stomachs of settlers in the Colorado Rockies, as well as the entire nation. Yet as we approach the hundredth anniversary of his death, the question lingers:

Was Packer guilty?

Born on November 21, 1842, Packer (anti-Alferd historians say his Allegheny County birth certificate reads "Alfred)
was a shoemaker when he enlisted in the U.S. 16th Infantry in
Winona, Minnesota, on April 22, 1862, but was honorably discharged on December 29 of that year in Fort Ontario, New
York, because of epilepsy. Other reports said he re-enlisted in
the Union army the following year, joining the 8th Iowa Cavalry, but again was forced to leave the service because of his
illness. In any event, the medical disability gave him a
$25-a-month pension.

After his military service, Packer drifted west. He probably
did a lot of mining, may have also worked on ranches and as a
hunter, guide, and scout, and is reported to have been a "jack
whacker" in Georgetown, Colorado, in 1872 and 1873. What
is certain is that he was in Provo, Utah, in the fall of 1873.

There, many people were casting an eye east toward Summit County, Colorado, where a new gold strike had been
discovered near the Blue River town of Breckenridge. Packer
said he knew the country and could guide the gold-seekers
but needed a grubstake as he was broke. Fellow Pennsylvanian Robert McGrew and Ireland-born George Tracy agreed to
split the advance, and in late November Packer led the party
— the exact number that left Provo is not certain — east. Others joined them, and by the time they reached the Colorado
border, the prospectors totaled twenty-one. In addition to
Packer, McGrew, and Tracy, the party included: Shannon Wilson Bell of Michigan, Mike Burke and John McCoy of Ireland,
Frenchman Jean "Frenchy" Cabazon, a Dr. Cooper from Scot-
land, Philadelphians George Driver and James Humphrey,
"Italian" Tom, O. D. Loutsenhizer of Ohio, Frank "Reddy"
Miller of Germany, "genial"[1] James McIntosh of Georgia,
Canadian James Montgomery, George "California" Noon of

Alfred Packer as he looked during his incarceration at the Colorado State Penitentiary in Cañon City. (Courtesy, Colorado State Archives)

San Francisco, West Virginian Preston Nutter, Israel Swan of Missouri, Dave Toll of Boston, and brothers Isaac and Tom Walker of parts unknown.

By January the so-called Party of 21 began to wish they had never left Utah. Out of food, they had begun to eat the chopped barley brought for their horses by the time they reached Colorado's San Juan region. They did not, however, turn back. Gold held a strong pull.

On January 21 help arrived near the confluence of the Uncompahgre and Gunnison Rivers near present-day Delta, Colorado, in the unlikely form of a party of Ute Indians. Once the Utes were convinced the white men were not homesteaders, merely prospectors, the Indian leader, who spoke English, told them it would be foolish to continue traveling because snow drifts made the mountain passes and trails impassable.

The Ute chief was Ouray. Son of a Tabeguache Ute mother and Jicarilla Apache father, he was born in 1833 at Abuiquiú, New Mexico, and raised there and in Taos. In addition to Ute and Apache, he could also speak Spanish and some English and is said to have been able to write his own name by the time he was twenty. During treaty negotiations in the 1860s, Indian Bureau officials gave him the title of Chief Ouray because of his help with translations and the fact that the Ute tribe had no recognizable leader. Because of his peacekeeping efforts in the 1860s and 1870s, not to mention his hospitality, he was called "The White Man's Friend."

Ouray lived up to his nickname by inviting the twenty-one prospectors to wait out the savage winter at his camp near present-day Montrose. He even allowed the men to stay in a cabin near the camp. Even more, he gave them flour and other supplies. Packer and the others recovered, restocked their meat supply, made repairs to their equipment, and rested their horses.

Despite Ouray's warnings to wait until spring, the white men became restless. Wagons couldn't handle the deep snow, but the men could travel on foot and perhaps bring a pack-horse along. In early February O. D. Loutsenhizer, Mike Burke, George Driver, and Isaac and Tom Walker left the encampment for the Los Pinos Indian Agency an estimated eighty-five to ninety miles away.[2] Located on Cochetopa Creek, a few miles from the junction of Los Pinos Creek or about forty miles from Saguache, the agency consisted of about a dozen log cabins and agent Charles Adams's house.

The Ute chief told the men to follow the Gunnison River, but the party lost its way during a blinding snowstorm. Out of food, they subsisted on rosebuds and wild berries until Loutsenhizer killed a wolf with a rifle or revolver. Later the men decided to split into two groups and go for help. Loutsenhizer traveled with Burke, and the two managed to kill a starving cow, eat the raw meat, and drink blood before staggering on. After a few days the two men stumbled into a hut occupied by James P. Kelly, the government cattle superintendent, and Kelly's assistant, Sidney Jocknick. Kelly and Jocknick cared for the two exhausted men before setting out in the storm to rescue Driver and the Walker brothers.

A few weeks later the five men continued their journey, finally reaching the Los Pinos Agency only because they saw light from a lantern Indian agent Charles Adams's wife just happened to have left on top of a cabin.

On February 9 the second part left the Ute encampment over Ouray's objections. Led by Packer, the party included Israel Swan, in his sixties and the oldest member of the party; Frank Miller, a butcher by trade; sixteen-year-old

George "California" Noon; redheaded Shannon Wilson Bell; and James Humphrey. They brought plenty of blankets and winter clothes, but, because Packer said the trip should take about seven days, only took a week's worth of food.

Preston Nutter and James Montgomery watched the six men and one packhorse disappear into the valley. Swan and Noon carried Winchester rifles or carbines, Bell had a hatchet and Miller a skinning knife. Packer, Nutter and Montgomery would later recall, apparently carried no weapon.

All that happened over the next two months will never be known, but on April 6, 1874, Packer came down from the mountains and limped into the agency's mess house. He carried live coals in a coffee pot (used to start fires) and a Winchester.

He was alone.

Eating breakfast at the time were Stephen A. Dole, agent Adams's secretary; Major James P. Downer, justice of the peace; and Herman Lauter, government clerk and constable. Packer told the men that he had become snowblind and that his feet became too sore to travel when not more than fifty miles from Los Pinos, so his five companions left him alone, promising to return with help. When they did not come back, he forced himself to travel, somehow managed to survive the wilderness, and made it to the agency.

Various stories exist as to his first meal. One said he could not eat anything without throwing up. Another said he asked for whiskey. Yet another said he became sick at the sight of red meat. The most outlandish is that while Packer told several men his harrowing account of starving, Chief Ouray shook his head and said, "Ugh. You too damn fat."[3]

Preston Nutter arrived at Los Pinos that same day. It took him two weeks to make the trip from Ouray's camp, but, of course, he left after a break in the weather. Nutter and Packer greeted each other warmly. The Winchester, Packer also explained, had been given him when the other five left in case he found any game. No one questioned his story.

"He did not have the appearance of having suffered from want of food," the *Saguache Chronicle* reported almost nine years later. "His face was bloated and he was apparently very healthy. His countenance was far from prepossessing, but no attention was paid to that at the time."[4]

Saying he was broke, Packer sold the Winchester and ammunition to James Downer for $10. He recovered quickly, and a few days later left for Saguache with Nutter, Dr. Cooper, and "Italian" Tom, who had also arrived from Ouray's winter camp. In Saguache, Packer found a friend in saloonkeeper James "Larry" Dolan. Packer would tend bar when Dolan was out, and the two men slept on the saloon's floor. Packer drank a lot, he ate a lot, and he spent money freely, buying a horse, saddle, and bridle from Otto Mears for $70.

Yet survivors of the trip from Utah remembered that Packer had been broke when they left Provo. They began to question how he got the Winchester. They also asked him about "Butcher Frank" Miller's skinning knife that Packer now had. Packer explained that the German butcher had left it in a tree, so he took it. Also questioned was why Packer had a pipe that had belonged to another member of the prospecting party.

On May 1 agent Charles Adams arrived in Saguache after a trip to Denver. Born Karl Adam Schwanbeck in Pomerania, German, Adams had served in the Union army during the Civil War and was appointed brigadier general of a Colorado territory militia district in 1870. In 1872 he took over as agent of the Los Pinos Agency. After hearing the suspicions voiced by the other prospectors — of the twenty-one, all but five had arrived at Saguache or Los Pinos by now — Adams questioned Packer himself.

The story was the same. Packer had been left behind because he was too ill to travel. They gave him a rifle. When he could walk again, he continued on to the agency, surviving on rosebuds and a rabbit that he killed.

Adams apparently believed him and asked him to serve as a guide. He wanted to send a search party after the other five. Packer agreed but again claimed to be broke. After Adams said he could find work for Packer at the agency, Packer agreed to go.

On the journey back to Los Pinos, Adams, his wife, and Packer encountered other survivors from the Utah expedition. One of these was Jean "Frenchy" Cabazon, who refused to believe that Bell, Humphrey, Miller, Noon, and Swan would have abandoned him in the mountains. The argument became so heated, the two men had to be separated.

Back at Los Pinos, Packer found fewer and fewer people believing his story. A later newspaper account would say that Packer finally broke down after two Indians arrived at the agency from a hunting trip. They carried strips of flesh in their hands. "White man's meat," they called it.

> It was in good condition, the white skin, which firmly adhered, convincing all present that it had been cut from a human being, apparently from the thigh. The strips were quite long and thin. When Packer caught sight of the flesh his face became livid, his breath came short, quick, and suddenly all strength left him, and with a low moan he sank to the floor.[5]

Maybe not. Another account says that Packer's retelling of his near-death experience became more and more confused, and that he began to suggest to Adams that some people, in extreme conditions, had been forced to eat human flesh. In either case, on May 8, Packer gave his first confession:

Old man Swan died first and was eaten by the other five persons, about ten days out from camp; four of five days later Humphrey died and was also eaten; he had about one hundred and thirty three dollars. I found the pocket-book and took the money. Some time afterwards while I was carrying wood, the Butcher was killed as the other two told me accidentally and he was eaten. Bell shot "California" with Swan's gun, and I killed Bell; shot him — covered up the remains, and took a large piece along. Then traveled fourteen days into the "Agency." Bell wanted to kill me, struck at me with his rifle, struck a tree and broke his gun.

I A. G. Packer do solemnly swear that the above statement is true and nothing but the truth So help me God.

A. G. Packer

Sworn to and subscribed before me this 8th day of May A.D. 1874. James P. Downer J.P.[6]

Many still didn't believe him, and Adams ordered a search party to the Lake Fork of the Gunnison River to find the remains. Reluctantly, Packer went along with Nutter, Cooper, McIntosh, constable Herman Lauter, "Indian Captain Billy," and two other Utes. Around Lake San Cristobal, Packer said he was lost. The country wasn't familiar to him.

The search party, however, found an old campsite, complete with a pillbox with Packer's name on it. The men decided that Packer had murdered his companions and disposed of the bodies in the lake. No bodies could be found, however, even after the men destroyed a beaver dam to lower the lake's water level. The searchers returned, and Adams arrested Packer on suspicion of murder and turned him over to Sheriff Amos Wall in Saguache.

Nothing happened until artist John A. Randolph, sketching scenes in the Uncompahgre Mountains for *Harper's Weekly*, came across the remains of five bodies in late August. His sketch, "The Remains of the Murdered Men. A COLORADO TRAGEDY," would appear in the October 17, 1874 edition of the newspaper. Another account, however, says three other men found the grisly sight. No matter who discovered the bodies, others, including Preston Nutter, rushed to the scene.

John A. Randolph's illustrations of the "Scene of the Tragedy" and "The Burial-Place" appeared in the October 17, 1874 edition of *Harper's Weekly*. (Author's Collection)

The grisly murder scene as depicted by artist John A. Randolph in the October 17, 1874 edition of *Harper's Weekly.* (Author's Collection)

Packer had not lied about cannibalism. Evidence supported that flesh had been consumed. The evidence also pointed to foul play. Nutter helped bury the bodies in a mass grave on what would become known as Dead Man's Gulch and Cannibal Plateau.

As word reached Saguache, Packer was placed in irons and confined in an adobe shack. Someone, he later said, gave him a penknife or a key made from a penknife, which he used to pick the locks and flee. A $5,000 reward was offered for his capture, but Packer would elude the law for almost nine years.

In January 1883 Packer was using the alias John Swartze. He had lost the first and fourth fingers of his left hand and wore a dental bridge that replaced two missing front teeth.

After a luckless prospecting venture along Spring Canyon in Wyoming with Clark Devoe and Devoe's father, Packer went to Fort Fetterman, near present-day Douglas, on a bender. When a waiter was too slow serving him, Packer drew a pistol and threatened to shoot. He was overpowered, however, and Albany County Deputy Sheriff Malcolm Campbell jailed him overnight, releasing him the next day when the waiter declined to press charges.

Packer, alias Swartze, continued to hang out in Wyoming and was still there that March when Jean "Frenchy" Cabazon stopped at John Brown's road ranch on La Prele Creek. Cabazon, who was peddling goods between Cheyenne and Fort Fetterman, was in his room when he recognized Packer's unmistakable high-pitched voice. One account says Cabazon approached Packer, who didn't recognize him. Another says Cabazon simply recognized Packer by staring through a hole in the wall and was too frightened to confront him. Certain that he had found the fugitive, Cabazon reported it to Malcolm Campbell.

Campbell wired Laramie and waited to hear back for instructions. Sheriff Louis Miller soon telegraphed Campbell to "Arrest Packer, alias John Swartze, at once, and take no chances." Campbell and his brother, Dan, rode to Wagonhound Creek, where Packer was staying in a cabin. On March 12 the lawmen arrived in a buckboard as Packer was stepping outside the cabin. They drew their guns and arrested him without incident. "He was surprised at the arrest, but soon adapted himself to the circumstances and made the best of it," the *Denver Republican* reported.[7]

Packer was transported to Laramie and then Cheyenne, where he was turned over to Hinsdale County (Colorado)

Sheriff Clair Smith on March 15. One day later the train carried Packer to Denver.

Although it was not generally known throughout the city that Packer would arrive last evening a crowd assembled at the Union depot some time before the train arrived, for no apparent reason but a morbid curiosity which impelled them to get a look at the man-eating murderer. That one look will undoubtedly be the foundation for innumerable stories of bloodshed and horror in years to come, and many of these stories will probably be exaggerated more or less with time.[8]

"Portly" Charles Adams soon arrived, and several lawmen escorted Packer to the Arapahoe County jail, where he answered a newspaper reporter's questions with "only short and curt replies."[9] Adams, Sheriff Smith, and Deputy United States Marshal Simon W. Cantril, who also happened to be a notary public, met with Packer in his cell, where he gave his second confession.

I, Alfred Packer, desire to make a true and voluntary statement in regard to the occurrences in Southern Colorado during the winter of 1873 to 1874. I wish to make it to General Adams because I have made one to him once before about the same matter.

When we left Ouray's camp we had about seven days of food for one man. We traveled two or three days and it came a storm. We came to a mountain, crossed a gulch and came onto another mountain, found the snow so deep, had to follow the mountain on the top and on about the fourth day we had only a pint of flour left. We followed the mountain until we came to the main range. I do not remember how many days we were traveling then; I think about ten days, living on rosebuds and pine gum, and some of the men were crying and praying.

Then we came over the main range. We camped twice on a stream which runs into a big lake, the second time just above the lake. The next morning we crossed the lake cut holes into the ice to catch fish, there were no fish so we tried to catch snails, the ice was thin, so some broke through. We crossed the lake and went into a grove of timber, all the men crying and one of them was angry — Swan asked me to go up and find out whether I could see something from the mountains — I took the gun and went up the hill. Found a gulch and came onto another mountain, found a big rosebush with buds sticking through the snow, but could see nothing but snow all around.

I was a kind of a guide for them but I did not know the mountains from that side. When I came back to camp after being gone nearly all day I found the red-headed man, Bell, who had acted crazy in the morning sitting near the fire roasting a piece of meat which he had cut out of the leg of the German butcher, Miller. The latter's body was lying the farthest off from the pile down the stream. His skull was crushed in with the hatchet, and the other three men were lying near the fire. They were cut in the forehead with the hatchet. Some had two and some three cuts.

I came within a rod of the fire when the man saw me. He got up with his hatchet in his hand and ran toward me, and I shot him sideways through the belly. He fell on his face, the hatchet fell forwards. I grabbed it and hit him in the top of the head. I camped that night at the fire, and sat up all night. The next morning I followed my tracks up the mountain, but I could not make it. The snow was too deep and I came back. I went sideways into a piece of pine timber, set up two stakes and covered it with pine boughs and made a shelter about three feet high. This was my camp until I came out.

I went back to the fire, covered the men up and fetched to the camp the piece of human flesh that was near the fire. I made a new fire near my camp, cooked the piece of meat and ate it. I tried every day to get away, but could not so I lived on the flesh of these men the bigger part of the sixty days I was out. Then the snow began to have a crust and I started out up the creek to a place where a big slide of yellowish clay seemed to come down the mountain. There I started up but got my feet wet and having only a piece of blanket around them I froze my feet under the toes and I camped before I reached the top, making a fire and staying all night.

The next day I made it to the top of the hill and a little over. I built a fire on top of a log and, on two logs close together, I camped. I cooked some of the flesh and carried it with me for food. I carried only one blanket. There was $70 among the men. I fetched it out with me and one gun. The red headed man, Bell, had a $50 bill in his pocket while all the others together had only $20. I had $20 myself. If there was any more money in the outfit I did not know of it and it remained there.

At the last camp just before I reached the agency I ate my last pieces of meat. This meat I cooked at the camp just before I started out and put it into a bag and carried the bag with me. I could eat but a little at a time. When I went out with the party from the agency to search for the bodies we came to the mountains overlooking the stream, but I did not want to take them further as I did not care to go back to the camp. If I had stayed in that vicinity longer I would have taken you (Mr. Adams) right to the place, but they advised me to go away.

Who "they" were, Packer would not tell.

When I was at the sheriff's cabin in Saguache, I was passed a key made out of a penknife blade with which I unlocked the irons about my feet and hands. I went to the Arkansas and worked all summer for John Gill, eighteen miles below Pueblo; then I rented Gilbert's ranch, still farther down the river, put in a crop of corn and sold it to John Gill and went to Arizona.

State of Colorado

County of Arapahoe

I, Al. Packer, of my own free will and voluntarily, do swear that the above statement is true, the whole truth and nothing but the truth, so help me God.

Signed Alferd Packer

Subscribed and sworn to before me this sixteenth day of March, 1883.

Sim W. Cantril, Notary Public[10]

The *Rocky Mountain News* ran the headline "A CANNIBAL'S CONFESSION," while the *Saguache Chronicle* called Packer "the Human Ghoul." Perhaps the most famous and sensational headline appeared in the *Denver Republican*:

HUMAN JERKED BEEF.
The Man Who Lived on Meat Out
From His Murdered
Victims.

———

The Fiend Who Became Very Corpu-
lent Upon a Diet of Human
Steaks.

———

A Cannibal Who Gnaws on the
Choice Cuts of His Fellow-
Man....

Sheriff Clair Smith proceeded with Packer west to Gunnison, where Judge M. B. Gerry suggested he leave the prisoner in the more secure steel cell of the county jail. Packer was held there. The district court convened on April 2, and four days later District Attorney John C. Bell moved for a murder indictment against Packer. He would be tried for the murder of Israel Swan not far from Lake San Cristobal in Lake City, a town that did not exist at the time of the incident. Why Bell did not include the murders of the other four men is not recorded.

The press, of course, already had Packer convicted after his Denver confession.

"THE CANNIBAL IS LYING," the *Denver Republican* reported, "As villainously in the last confession as he did in his first. He could not brook cross examination, and General

Adams was compelled to be content with his recital of the story. Whenever he would call the murderer's attention to the facts, the murderer would flare up, tremble and go on with his story. Neither General Adams nor Sheriff Smith takes any stock in Packer and his stories."[11]

The *Rocky Mountain News* noted that "It is more certain than ever that Packer MURDERED THE MEN for purposes of robbery and to eat their flesh."[12] While the *Saguache Chronicle* said: "The gibbet will surely be his portion."[13]

Elsewhere in the *Republican*:

> That is a ghastly crime with which the man Packer, now confined in the Arapahoe county jail, is charged. Not only is the blood of five human beings upon his hands, but he confesses that he subsisted upon their flesh for sixty days. That he is guilty of wilful [sic] and premeditated murder there is no doubt. That he committed the crime in order to obtain possession of the money which his comrades carried is equally certain. That it is susceptible of proof that he committed these murders before the party was out of provisions, and when almost within sight of the settlements we firmly believe. "An eye for an eye and a tooth for a tooth" is the Divine law and the good people of Hinsdale county will execute it.[14]

At least Packer would get his day in court.

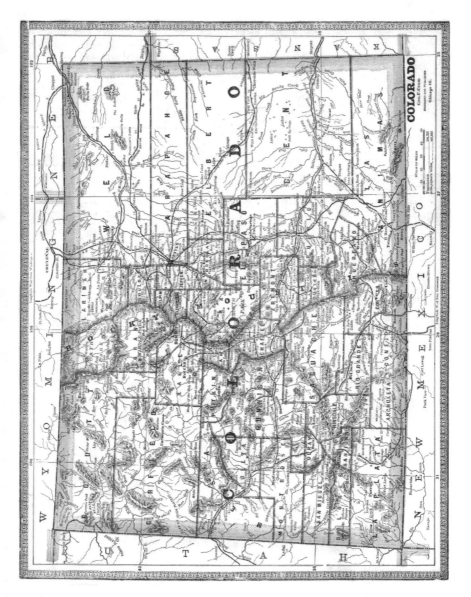

The Colorado of Alfred Packer's trial era can be seen in this 1886 map of the state.
(Author's Collection)

Trial

Prospecting had begun around Lake San Cristobal around 1871, and a mining camp was founded about three years later only two and one-half miles from Cannibal Plateau. At an elevation of 8,672 feet, Lake City boasted a population of five hundred in 1876 that skyrocketed to three thousand within two years. The Denver & Rio Grande Railroad began grading a line to the mining town in the fall of 1881 but soon stopped, and the first train would not reach Lake City until August 15, 1889. Lake City's population began to decline, but it still was home to one thousand to fifteen hundred folks in 1883.

Lake City lawyer J. Warner Mills would serve as second chair to District Attorney John C. Bell, while Packer would be defended by Aaron Heims and A. J. Miller. On Saturday, April 7, the defense quickly objected that the court lacked jurisdiction to try the case, but Judge M. B. Gerry ruled that with the 1873 Brunot treaty, the Utes had ceded the rights to the San Juan country, making the site of the crime public domain, so he denied Heims's motion, to which the lawyer took exception. Heims also asked for a continuance, which was also denied and exception taken. Court was then adjourned until Monday, April 9.

The *voir dire* process took until 4 p.m. Monday, as lawyers interviewed fifty-six or fifty-eight potential jurors before filling the jury box with J. C. DuBois, David Edgar, Charles Festanmacher, G. W. Wood, Patrick McEnany, John Henderson, Robert Mitchell, H. C. Huston, N. P. Meserve, Henry Snider, Herman Meyer, and J. P. Titsworth. Edgar was chosen foreman, and George Sullivan was appointed the jury's bailiff.

The prosecution would argue that Packer murdered the five men with a hatchet for profit. The defense stuck by

Packer's Denver confession, that he had killed Shannon Bell in self-defense and had to eat human flesh to stay alive. Again, transcripts do not exist, and the testimony is taken from reporter M. M. Lewis's account in the *Lake City Silver World*. In Lewis's article, "the questions [were] merely indicated by the answers, exceptions, etc, being omitted...."[15]

The first witness was Preston Nutter, who over the next two days recalled the journey from Utah and finding Swan's body and the other corpses in August 1874.

[Swan's] body was...almost decaying, lying with the head up the creek, the head covered with the corner of a blanket and a wound cut through the blanket into the skull. I lifted the blanket, and blood and hair stuck to it. No other indications of violence.

The flesh was not cut from the body. The clothing was cut and ripped up through the seams and crosswise and thrown on the body. The body showed no indications of having been disturbed since death....

The bodies were found under a steep, high bluff. There was a dense growth of willows and other trees, and it was so dark that I could not for some time discern the bodies. It was about 10 o'clock in the morning.[16]

The other bodies, Nutter testified, showed hatchet wounds, except Humphrey's, whose skull had been crushed. Miller had been decapitated. Nutter illustrated the positions of the bodies near the remains of a campfire and swore that none of the bodies had been disturbed since death. A pillbox given to Packer by Dr. Cooper was also found at the camp. The box had Packer's name on it.

Nutter also contradicted Packer's account that game was scarce in the region. "I had no trouble killing mountain sheep and beaver," he said. He related Packer's confession to Adams at the agency and added that when Packer was asked "why they did not cut enough flesh from the first victim to last and save killing so many of the party," he had no answer.

Under cross-examination, Nutter said that he and Montgomery had "poor success" on two hunting outings while at Ouray's camp. He said that Packer's party took seven or eight days' provisions but that it was a ten-day trip from the Ute encampment to Lake City alone. He then admitted that he had never prospected in the San Juan country, but that he and Montgomery had survived for seven days on fifty pounds of flour once in Idaho.

Agent Charles Adams recalled his May 1, 1874 meeting with Packer and the subsequent investigation. Packer told Adams that he had been given money by a Saguache blacksmith, but after checking that out, he called Packer in for an interview and asked again what had become of Bell, Humphrey, Miller, Noon, and Swan. Packer replied:

"I have nothing more to add."

"Not in regard to the money?"

"No."

"Then I will tell you, you have lied to me. Kinkaid, the blacksmith, gave you no money. I ask again where did you get the money? I do not wish to hunt for dead men. I believe those men are dead, and you might as well tell the truth. If the men died you are more to be pitied than blamed. You know the facts and I do not want to send a party out if they are not living."

He sat silent for a time, then said:

"It is not the first time that people have had to eat each other, when hungry."

"No," I replied, "I have heard of such occurrences. Is that the case here?"

He seemed excited; tears filled his eyes, and he said:

"I would tell the whole story, but I am afraid of the boys."

I told him he need not be afraid; if he told the truth he would be perfectly safe.

Adams then recalled Packer's first confession. After the first searches, Adams said, he advised the justice of the peace to send Packer to Saguache for the suspect's own safety. "I did not see Packer again until a month ago," Adams testified.

Packer's Denver confession was entered into evidence. As far as the contradictions between the two statements, Adams said Packer explained: "He said he was excited; that he wanted to tell the straight story but the other came to his mind first."

Cross-examination was brief, with the attorneys hitting on the point that Packer had been excited during his 1874 confession and "did not know exactly," Adams said, "what he was saying." On the other hand, in the prosecution's redirect, Adams said Packer "spoke in such a rational collected way that I thought it was true. If he had not seemed perfectly rational I would not have believed his story then."

Otto Mears followed Adams on the stand, testifying that when Packer bought the horse and gear, he spotted a draft in his pocketbook. George Tracy also said Packer was broke when the prospectors left Utah. Then Hesekiah Musgrave, who lived on Carnero Creek in 1874, was called to the stand.

Musgrave, who first admitted that he had not heard Nutter's testimony, said that while on the trail in August 1874 he met a party of artists who said they had found five dead bodies under a cliff. He went to the site and found:

Three bodies were lying near together and two off a short distance. They had been killed by some sharp instrument.

I noticed the flesh had been cut from the breast and limbs.

Three bodies were not more than three feet apart, other two six or eight feet away.

One had the head mashed, appeared as though there might have been a struggle. The others seemed to have been killed by a single blow.

Musgrave said the bodies did not appear to have been moved and that he had not touched the bodies, but that the artists had been there before him and that he was there for no longer than ten minutes.

Perhaps the most outlandish testimony came from Herman Lauter. After rehashing earlier statements, he recalled two incidents that happened during the search party Packer had guided.

All the boys were afraid of Packer. When out with him alone I found a knife on his person and demanded it. He made a rush at me with it and I grabbed his hand and took it from him.

It was a skinning-knife, and was secreted on his bare body. This was the fourth day out.

On the way, after eating dinner, I was taken suddenly ill with cramps, as if poisoned.

> Nutter and I were attending team, and I left pris-
> oner alone before dinner. I was very ill.

The defense attacked Lauter's claims. The constable admitted that he and Packer were alone, therefore no one else witnessed the alleged knife attack.

Was Lauter lying? Packer, naturally, said he was, and the passage alluding to an attempted poisoning is hard to believe.

Los Pinos Agency secretary Herman Lueders and secretary Stephen A. Dole repeated earlier testimony, before James Dolan remembered Packer's spending habits in the Saguache saloon. Among Dolan's statements:

> He played "freeze-out" for drinks with the boys and one day was stuck for $37....

> One afternoon he spent $37, and he played cards with me for drinks at other times amounting to $7 or $8....

> At one time when talking about money matters he said if I was short he'd loan me $800. I think he had that much and more. I did not take the money.

Next, Sheriff Clair Smith said that Packer's manner was quiet during his Denver confession, but that once or twice he got excited and "jumped to his feet when telling the story of killing Bell and eating flesh."

James P. Downer then told of buying the Winchester from Packer for $10 but said he saw no other money on him. He felt sorry for Packer because both came from Pennsylvania, and he said he had served with a Packer relative, W. F. Packer, in the legislature in 1851. The last witness on Tuesday was Undersheriff John Davis whose testimony led to the prosecution entering the 1873 treaty into evidence as proof that the court had jurisdiction to try the case.

Court was adjourned until 9 a.m. Wednesday.

The last prosecution witness was Ohioan O. D. Loutsenhizer, who briefly testified that Packer asked the other prospectors about money. Cross-examination was brief, and the prosecution rested its case at 9:20 a.m.

Loutsenhizer then became the first witness to testify for the defense and described his own ordeal when he, Driver, Burke, and the Walker brothers tried to reach Los Pinos from the Ute encampment. His group also had provisions for eight days but were in the wilderness for twenty-one. He shot two jackrabbits with a Colt Navy revolver, and the men had nothing else to eat but "joint-rushes, water-cresses, and rose-buds" until killing the wolf and later the cow.

Packer testified on his own behalf. After being sworn in, he said he wanted to make a statement and not be interrupted, and he wanted to stand while talking. Judge Gerry granted both requests. Packer also asked that Downer, Lauter, Mears, Dolan, Tracy, and Adams step inside the railing. Only Dolan, Tracy, and Downer were in the courtroom, and they came forward with Gerry's permission. Speaking rapidly, he said he had worked in the Bingham Canyon mines in Utah, was "leaded," and almost died before he came to Provo.

"His [harangue] in many respects was similar to that of [President James A. Garfield assassin Charles] Guiteau," the *Silver World* reported, "and his thinly disguised falsehoods and occasional displays of his native fiendish spirit left the same impressions as did the Washington criminal's exhibition."[17]

For nearly two hours, Packer testified:

Went down the valley to Sandy, where I heard that a party was preparing to go to the San Juan county, Colorado. I had lived at Breckenridge and Fairplay a year and a half before, and wanted to return to Colorado. Met McGrew and Tracy. Told Bob wanted to come through but had no money. McGrew agreed to take me for $25, and I was to assist in camp and care for team. Started in September [actually November, but a lot of witnesses had their dates wrong nine years after the fact]. Boys kept falling in until there were 21 in party in different messes. Bob had four-horse team, McCoy mule team, Tracy a horse. Run short of provisions near Green river, and the boys growled. I growled for one. Not much of a crank, but I growled. Game scarce. Talked about eating horse flesh. We proposed to Bob to kill a crippled horse. He said he could eat a fine little mare he had. Don't remember about money matters. I had $50 when I paid fare.

We were all jealous and out of food. I was not the only one that growled. I was jealous of Bob. Nutter and I got on raft and run on to island in Green river. After party crossed, Driver and Frenchy quarreled. First hard words. I told boys I'd been on Blue and Grand rivers, trapped at Breckenridge. Wanted to go up Grand river and make Breckenridge. Indians came whooping and yelling after us. We prepared for them. We went on nearer Ouray's camp. Ouray invited us to his camp to give Indians a chance to trade. There were hard feelings among the party. This was about the 25th or 27th of January. My birthday, the 21st, was a few days before. I felt jealous but said nothing. Company concluded to stay some time and Swan and I built a shanty of brush without leaves with fire in center. Others did the same. One Sibley tent and two wagon covers in the party. Nothing said about money. I got a horse of Nutter and went to Ouray's camp for supplies. Had to pay $20 a hundred for flour. Got two or three goats, coffee sugar and barley of Indians. Swan divided up with the other boys.

First party [Loutsenhizer's] started to agency. Were generally sociable. Dr. Cooper cursed McCoy and threatened to scalp him. Old man Swan was with me. They never offered him wagon cover. Nutter and Tracy stopped in the tent. Six of us concluded to start for the agency, and follow the other party. We packed utensils and provisions enough for seven days — borrowed horse that was sent back next day. Bell and Noon each had guns. Two days after we struck snow we had only one pint of flour left. A horrible snow storm filled our trail so we could not follow the gulches. We thought agency under mountains and that could see valley from any ridge. Followed one ridge three or four days, when George Noon gave up his moccasins (raw-hide). We burned off the hair, cooked and eat them. Matches gave out. Swan carried fire in a coffee pot, and wore socks on his hands. We carried his pack. After four or five days Bell gave up his moccasins. We camped, and right there was the first cranky work. Noon stepped on Bell's foot, and Bell "cussed" him. Swan urged them not to quarrel. Next morning we started without breakfast. Second day we found a big patch of rosebuds. Reaching a log under a stream, we camped. Five or six days after Bell's moccasins were eaten I gave up mine.

We wished for salt — the last dying word was salt. We traveled down the range. Noon led, and the snow was so deep that we concluded to follow the ridge, and after one day concluded it was so cold we'd freeze to death. There was no wood. We expected all the time to look over and see the agency.

Swan had give out. We prayed and cried. Swan made a good prayer. I tried to pray. Before we came down where the bodies were found we prayed and cried all the time. Bell wouldn't say a word for two or three days. He was a big man, red headed, and his eyes bunged out.

Packer showed (using a map, perhaps) how the party came down, likely from Red Mountain, despite deep snow, to the Lake Fork of the Gunnison, and to Cannibal Plateau. He continued:

We were eating pine gum and swallowing it, getting weaker and weaker. I don't know that this is the stream (Lake Fork) where the bodies were found.

We camped at a big pine root that had been burned. That night we had a prayer meeting. Our whole wish was for salt. We camped near a lake — it looked like a lake. Found some buds. Next morning Miller broke trail to lake, and broke through the ice, but could find no fish. Noon cut through the ice with hatchet near the edge and tried to find snails, but there were none — only muck. Did not venture far out on the ice.

Then we traveled down the stream and found buds. We camped again. Then we gave up to die. I gave up to die. We could not go farther. Was cold and stormy. Swan was the weakest man in the outfit. We was clean gone, we couldn't go no farther. Well, that settled it! I thought I'd go to the top of the mountain and look for the agency! Swan asked me to go. They said they'd pray for me and have a good fire when I returned. Took gun and used it for walking stick. Found some rosebuds that saved my life — could never have got back but for them. When I returned it was getting dark. Bell was sitting there near the fire. When he saw me he come for me with the hatchet. He didn't say anything, but gritted his teeth. I took aim — no, raised my gun and shot him right there (through the abdomen). He fell forward, and I took the hatchet and struck him in the head — forehead. Did not crush the skull. Bell had cut piece of flesh from Miller and was roasting it.

I then called to the other boys, but got no answer. Found they were dead. They were struck with the hatchet. Bell owned the hatchet. Miller was hit three times I think with the hatchet. Swan was struck once in the head.

That same night I took blankets and covered them up. I set there all night. Next morning the bodies were froze. I took kettle and started away, but had to go back. I went into the pine built a fire and cooked some of the flesh. Right there was my last feeling. I eat that meat, and that's what hurts me, and has for nine years.

I can't tell how long I was there. I was perfectly happy and contented. Did not suffer — did not think of the agency. I just wanted to sleep. But after awhile fear came back to me. I seemed to think of the agency, and I started twice with fire in coffee pot and no provisions, and both times came back. In March the snow began to have a crust. I went back to the bodies and cut off some flesh with the butcher knife, cooked it and filled a cartridge sack to carry with me.

When I cut flesh with Miller's knife I found pocket-book with $70, and I took the money. Perhaps it was wrong, but I took it. I had $20 myself. I then started with the coffee pot and went up the mountain. That evening I froze my feet before I got fire to burning. Next morning started to go down a gulch — snow crust too soft, and went back to camp-fire. Tried to tie sticks on my feet to walk on snow, but couldn't. I eat rose buds and little of the flesh. Traveled down to where I brought Nutter's party. Don't know how many days I traveled. When I camped three-fourths of a mile from the agency I had three pieces of meat and some rosebuds. Next morning when I saw the agency I put my coffee pot and fire down and carried my gun in. The wouldn't allow me to eat as much as I wanted. Sold gun to Downer for $10 — that made me $100.

I then went to Saguache. There was no accommodations there. Larry Dolan asked me to sleep with him, and I did. Business wasn't flush, you bet!

Dolan bought oysters and canned fruit. I slept with him. When he went up to Mears store I kept bar. When I wanted a drink I went and took it, whether I paid or not. Was there with Dolan six days when Adams drove up.

Seventh day I gave Larry $50 bill I took from Bell and he gave me change. Gen. Adams said he'd give me work.

Dolan swore I lost $37 at freeze-out. I say Packer never played a game of freeze-out in Larry Dolan's place, and I will prove it by the deputy sheriff of Saguache. Larry spent more money with me than I did with him.

Then, "in a rambling way," he denied the testimony of Dolan, Mears, and Lauter. Dolan's charges of Packer's gambling were lies. "Dolan attested that he did not know what a $50 gold note was, except it's 'yaller'!" Mears was lying when he testified that he saw a Wells Fargo check in his pocketbook, and Lauter's story of disarming the knife from Packer was ludicrous. "If I go to kill a man with a knife I'd cut both his hands off before he'd get my knife," Packer said, adding, "You bet if I'd struck him with a knife it'd made him cramp. Lauter said he got cramped, as much to say I poisoned him."

His first confession at Los Pinos "was a deliberate lie," and several parties — again unnamed — advised him to leave.

It probably didn't help his cause, however, when he told of his experiences while being held prisoner in Saguache. For a pastime, he would catch blackbirds, cut a hole through paper and stick it over their heads, then release them "to frighten the other birds." In addition to the penknife given him to escape, Packer said he was also supplied with whiskey and provisions.

He closed his statement with: "Now, gentlemen, there is the whole story, and I'm going to quit, for it ain't interesting what I've done since then, unless you want to hear it."[18]

Now questioned by his attorneys, Packer said he remained at the agency two or three days before he was interrogated and that Adams told him "I'd better confess — that the boys were hot." He again denied Lauter's knife story, saying that he was unarmed while with the search party and that Miller's knife had been taken from him at Los Pinos. He said that his Denver confession was the true one and that he had little money, after spending most of what he had on whiskey and tobacco in Saguache, when he was searched.

Under cross-examination, Packer said he couldn't explain why he shot Bell. "If it was to-day, I'd strike him with the gun," he said before court was adjourned until the afternoon.

John Bell fired off his questions quickly when court reconvened, "hoping to confuse the defendant and thereby elicit information not otherwise obtainable, with however, partial success only."[19]

Packer conceded that he had trapped before and knew how to catch mink and beaver in Colorado, but added that he "saw nothing to trap on the trip." He also denied that Dr. Cooper ever gave him medicine or a pillbox.

In describing the Shannon Bell shooting, Packer said: "The snow was probably 18 inches deep where Bell fell when shot. Hatchet did not sink into the snow where it fell. I struck Bell just above the right eye on the forehead; I struck him in an instant after he fell. It was all done in a flash. He did not speak. He made an effort to speak — raised up and straightened out. He laid down on the snow on his face."

The district attorney quickly countered, asking Packer how could he have struck Bell on the forehead with the hatchet when he fell facedown. The *Silver World* reported that Packer became "badly mixed" and could give "no tangible answer."

To explain why he had lied in his first confession, Packer said he "was young and didn't know as much as now, and if I had it to do over again should have done different; was bothered by everybody and didn't know what I ought to do."

Packer also explained the positions of the bodies: "Bell had killed all but the butcher as they lay and the butcher had started to run and was overtaken by Bell and struck the blow with the hatchet. He was weak. We were all dead on our feet."

In all, Packer had spent six hours on the stand.

Downer and Nutter were then recalled as defense witnesses, with the justice of the peace saying the 1874 confession had been voluntary and the prospector recalling a bone found near the camp. "It had a hole through it as if made by a bullet." The prosecution was arguing that Packer had killed the five with a hatchet, while Packer argued he had killed only Shannon Bell, and that he had shot him. However, Nutter, likely under cross-examination by the district attorney, added that he "Was confident [the bone] could not have come from a person's body."

Thus, the defense rested. District Attorney Bell gave his closing argument, followed by defense arguments by Heims and Miller. J. Warner Mills closed for the state, and at about 7 p.m. Thursday, April 12, Judge Gerry charged the jury. Two hours later the jury reported no unanimous verdict, so court was adjourned until 9 a.m. Friday.

On the first ballot, the jury voted eleven-to-one to convict. On the final ballot, the lone juror sided with the others. On Friday morning, jury foreman David Edgar reported the verdict to the court.

STATE OF COLORADO.

County of Hinsdale,

In the District Court of the 7th Judicial District within and for the said county of Hinsdale, in the State of Colorado.

The People of Colorado, Plaintiff,

vs.

Alferd Packer, Defendant,

We the jury in the above entitled cause, find the above defendant, Alferd Packer, guilty as charged in the indictment, and that the killing charged in said indictment was premeditated.

Packer stood to face Judge Gerry, who asked for any reason why the court should not pass sentence. Packer's reply: "I don't feel guilty of the act I am charged with. That is all."

"What is your age?" Gerry asked.

"Thirty-four the 21st of next January," he lied. He would turn forty-one in November.

"Is your correct name Alferd Packer?"

"It is. My name was [tattooed] on my arm when I was 13 years old." Another fabrication. He had obviously been tattooed after joining the 16th Infantry when he was nineteen.

Packer said he had no family, and Gerry pronounced sentence:

> It becomes my duty as the Judge of this Court to enforce the verdict of the jury rendered in your case, and impose on you the judgment which the law fixes as the punishment of the crime you have committed. It is a solemn, painful duty to perform. I would to God the cup might pass from me! You have had a fair and impartial trial. You have been faithfully and earnestly defended by able counsel. The presiding Judge of this Court, upon his oath and his conscience, has labored to be honest and impartial in the trial of your case, and in all doubtful questions presented you have had the benefit of the doubt.
>
> A jury of twelve honest citizens of the county have set in judgment on your case, and upon their oaths

they find you guilty of willful and premeditated murder — a murder revolting in all its details. In 1874 you
in company with five companions passed through this
beautiful mountain valley where stands the town of
Lake City. At this time the hand of man had not
marred the beauties of nature. The picture was fresh
from the hand of the Great Artist who created it. You
and your companions camped at the banks of a stream
as pure and beautiful as ever traced by the finger of
God upon the bosom of the earth. Your every sur-
rounding was calculated to impress upon your heart
and nature the omnipotence of Deity, and the helpless-
ness of your own feeble life. In this goodly favored
spot you conceived your murderous designs.

You and your victims had had a weary march, and
when the shadow of the mountains fell upon your little party and night drew her sable curtain around you,
your unsuspecting victims lay down on the ground and
were soon lost in the sleep of the weary; and when
thus sweetly unconscious of danger from any quarter,
and particularly from you, their trusted companion;
you cruelly and brutally slew them all. Whether your
murderous hand was guided by the misty light of the
moon, or the flickering blaze of the camp fire, you can
only tell. No eye saw the bloody deed performed, no
ear save your own caught the groans of your dying victims. You then and there robbed the living of life, and
then robbed the dead of the reward of honest toil
which they had accumulated; at least so say the jury.
To other sickening details of your crime I will not refer.
Silence is kindness. I do not say these things to harrow
your soul, for I know you have drunk the cup of

bitterness to its very dregs, and wherever you have gone, the sting of your conscience and the goadings of remorse have an avenging Nemesis which have followed you at every turn in life and painted afresh for your contemplation the picture of the past. I say these things to impress upon your mind the awful solemnity of your situation and the impending doom which you cannot avert. Be not deceived, God is not mocked, for whatsoever a man soweth that shall he also reap. You, Alfred Packer, sowed the wind; you must now reap the whirlwind. Society cannot forgive you for the crime you have committed. It enforces the old Masonic law of a life for a life, and your life must be taken as the penalty of your crime. I am but the instrument of society to impose the punishment which the law provides. While society cannot forgive it will forget. As the days come and go, the story of your crimes will fade from the memory of men.

With God it is different. He will not forget, but will forgive. He pardoned the dying thief on the cross. He is the same God today as then — a God of love and of mercy, of long suffering and for kind forbearance; a God who tempers the wind to the shorn lamb, and promises rest to all the weary and heart-broken children of men; and it is to this God I commend you.

Close up your ears to the blandishments of hope. Listen not to its flattering promises of life; but prepare for the dread certainty of death. Prepare to meet thy God; prepare to meet that aged father and mother of whom you have spoken and who still love their dear boy.

For nine long years you have been a wanderer upon the face of the earth, bowed and broken in spirit; no home; no loves; no ties to bind you to earth. You have been indeed, a poor, pitiable waif of humanity. I hope and pray that in the spirit land to which you are so fast and surely drifting, you will find that peace and rest for your weary spirit which this world cannot give.

Alfred Packer, the judgment of this Court is that you be removed from hence to the jail of Hinsdale County, and there be confined until the 19th day of May, A.D. 1883, and that on said 19th day of May 1883, you be taken from thence by the Sheriff of Hinsdale County, to a place of execution for this purpose, at some point within the corporate limits of the town of Lake City, in the said County of Hinsdale, and between the hours of 10 A.M. and 3 P.M. of said day, you then and there, by the said Sheriff, be hung by the neck until you are dead, dead, dead, and may God have mercy upon your soul.[20]

It was a fine speech, flowery, religious, typical of the period. What became legend, however, were two apocryphal statements attributed to the judge. One was that he called Packer a man-eating son of a bitch, wagged a finger at the convicted man, and raged that there were only seven Democrats in the county and that Packer had eaten five of them and thus he would hang as a warning against reducing Colorado's Democratic population. The other legendary sentence was that Gerry called Packer a Republican cannibal and would sentence him to hell if the statutes allowed it.

Again, the defense moved for a new trial, offering several arguments that Gerry rejected. Next, Packer's lawyers informed the judge of their intent to appeal to the Colorado Supreme Court and, if necessary, the U.S. Supreme Court. They asked the judge to order the clerk and stenographer to prepare transcripts at the county's expense. Gerry rejected this as well, and the two attorneys agreed to pay for the transcript themselves.

Construction of the gallows began shortly, but a quirk in Colorado law would give Packer a reprieve.

Aftermath

For three years Packer sat in the county jail in Gunnison, selling his photograph to tourists for fifty cents a pop, while his lawyers were busy at work.

In 1875 a man and his three sons had been murdered in Denver. Three men were charged with the crime, but the attorney for one of the accused, future Colorado governor and senator Charles S. Thomas, told his client to plead guilty. Once the plea had been entered, Thomas pointed out that the 1870 territorial legislature had ruled that in murder cases the jury had to prove premeditation before a death sentence could be pronounced. Because Thomas's client had pleaded guilty, no jury could be impaneled and therefore his client could not be hanged. The judge reluctantly agreed, and Thomas's client was sentenced to life in prison.

Five years after Colorado was admitted into the union in 1876, the state legislature repealed the 1870 law and adopted a measure that allowed for death sentences after guilty pleas. The 1881 legislature also repealed a similar statue regarding larceny.

The blunder was that in repealing the previous laws, the state legislature forgot to add a "savings clause" to the old statutes. Therefore the old laws were nonexistent. In 1883 the state Supreme Court overturned the larceny conviction of one man because of the lack of the "savings clause," and one month after Packer's trial, criticized the legislature but was forced to free a murderer because the 1870 murder law had also been repealed and the 1881 law could not be made retroactive.

Citing the precedent, Packer's lawyers appealed. The state's highest court overturned the lower court's verdict but did not discharge Packer. Packer had been convicted only of the murder of Israel Swan. The lack of a "savings clause" forced the Supreme Court to set aside the 1883 decision, but Packer could be tried on five counts of manslaughter because that law had not been repealed.

On July 31, 1886, Packer, now represented by Thomas C. Brown, was arraigned in the district court in Gunnison on five charges of manslaughter. He pleaded not guilty, and the five cases were consolidated. Prosecuting this time was new district attorney Herschel Millard Hogg, assisted by, once again, J. Warner Mills. Much of the testimony was the same as during the 1883 trial, but Packer didn't help matters by cursing his so-called enemies and testimony from the previous trial. The jury found him guilty of five counts of manslaughter.

On August 5, before being sentenced, Packer told the judge: "I expect a [maximum] sentence of forty years. You must give it to me under the circumstances, but won[']t you do this — won[']t you sentence me to forty years for the killing of Bell? Don't say anything about the others. Just give me all for one man."

The judge, named Harris or Harrison, replied: "I would like to if I could, Mr. Packer, but the law will not permit it."[21] Packer was then sentenced to forty years at hard labor in the state penitentiary in Canon City — "a Punishment," a *Rocky Mountain News* headline scolded, "Inadequate To His Crime."[22]

Packer, convict number 1389, arrived at the prison later that day. A model prisoner, he worked as a harness maker, carved canes, made horsehair belts, and earned the praise of Warden C. P. Hoyt. Appeals of his second conviction were denied because of the failure to produce transcripts of the Gunnison trial. The last rejection came on June 19, 1899, but petitions for Packer's parole were already circulating, and he remained in the news.

The *Denver Sunday Times* reported in 1900:

Whether Alfred Packer is justly punished may always be a question in the minds of some. Interest in his case will never abate. It is now nearly seventeen years since he was captured, tried and sentenced to death for a murder committed twenty-six years ago. Through a technicality he was saved from the gallows, and fourteen years ago he entered the Colorado state penitentiary at Canon City with a sentence of forty years against him, eight years for each of five alleged cases of murder, the jury having found him guilty of manslaughter on each count. Since that time Packer's case has been almost continuously before either the supreme court or the state board of pardons. While he has practically no means of his own, the notoriety that would come to anyone who might get him out of prison has been sufficient to attract many lawyers, and in this way the prisoner has had constantly the best of legal advice, and all that shrewd minds could do has been done. But so far the effort has been unavailing. Governor after governor has declined to grant the pardon sought, while nothing has been presented to the supreme court that would warrant that body in opening the case anew.[23]

Denver Post reporter Polly Pry began pushing for Packer's parole or pardon. Ironically, parole would finally come thanks to Charles S. Thomas, the 1875 lawyer whose legal work in a Denver murder case paved the way for Packer's second trial. As governor, Thomas had refused to parole or pardon Packer, but on January 7, 1901, the day before Thomas would leave office and James B. Orman would be inaugurated, Thomas granted Packer a parole that stipulated he remain in Colorado for the rest of his life.

Packer left prison with a new suit, a one-way railroad ticket to Denver, and $400. He stayed in Denver a few months, thanking Polly Pry and his fans at the *Post*, then moved to Littleton, later to Sheridan and, in 1905, to Deer Creek Canyon. In July 1906 Colorado game warden Charles Cash found Packer ill and took him to Cash's mother-in-law's cabin. There, the widow Van Alstine and Cash's wife would care for Packer, who suffered several epileptic seizures, over the next several months.

At 6:50 p.m. Wednesday, April 23, 1907, Packer, surrounded by Van Alstine and the Cashes, died.

"His face changed," Mrs. Cash told the *Denver Post*. "His face changed before he died. It began to change on Wednesday afternoon. A light came into it and it looked like a field looks when the grass waves in the wind and the sun comes out from behind the clouds. He lay in bed all the afternoon smiling, smiling like a child that dreams in his sleep. And he had never smiled much before."[24]

Not all the newspapers were so kind. The headline in the April 27 edition of the *Rocky Mountain News* read: "ALFRED PACKER, CONVICTED OF MURDER AND CANNIBALISM, NOW FACES HIS GOD."

A week before his death, Packer had written Governor Henry Buchtel: "I am dying, and I am innocent of crime. I wish to meet my Maker without a shadow hanging over me, and so I ask that I be given an unconditional pardon for the crime of which I was convicted. I have asked nothing in the past, but I want to die clear in the opinion of my fellow man."[25] Buchtel took no action.

Although the *Littleton Independent* reported Packer's dying words as "I am not guilty of the charge,"[26] he apparently made no deathbed statement. He was buried in a plain casket on April 24 in the Littleton cemetery.

A legend like Packer, of course, never really dies. Ken Hodgson wrote a wickedly funny first-person novel told from Packer's point of view, *Lone Survivor*, published in 2000. There have been specials, documentaries, cookbooks, restaurants, even a musical about the man-eater. Not to mention investigations trying to clear his name or prove his guilt.

Scientists descended on Cannibal Plateau in 1988 and dug up what they believed was Shannon Bell's skeleton. After the discovery of a hole in the hipbone, some argued it was a bullet hole and thus proved Packer's innocence. Others said rodents had gnawed the hole. Early in 2001 Mesa State College scientists examined soil and cloth from the massacre site and uncovered a piece of lead many believed came from a bullet.

That, Packer defenders said, proved that Packer had killed only Bell, and only in self-defense. Unless, Packer detractors can argue, Packer shot Bell, then brained him with the hatchet after murdering the others.

Who knows?

Chapter Notes

Primary sources: *The Case of Alfred Packer The Man-Eater: An Unsolved Mystery of the West* (University of Denver Press, 1952) by Paul H. Gantt; *Alfred Packer: The True Story of the Man-Eater* (B&B Printers, 1963) by Robert W. "Red" Fenwick; selected papers from the Alfred Packer Collection, Colorado State Archives; and various editions of the *Denver Post*, *Denver Republican*, *Denver Sunday Times*, *Denver Times*, *Georgetown Courier*, *Lake City Silver World*, *Littleton Independent*, *Rocky Mountain News*, and *Saguache Chronicle*.

1. *Saguache Chronicle*, March 23, 1883.
2. From Ken Hodgson, whose Carl Hiassen-like novel, *Lone Survivor*, was a first-person account of Packer: "Given all of the twists and turns to go around mountains that now have neat holes blasted through them, and rivers you don't have to look for a shallow spot to cross, I'd estimate 85 to 90 miles. Doesn't seem like much of a trip these days, does it?"
3. *Rocky Mountain News*, April 27, 1907.
4. *Saguache Chronicle*, March 23, 1883.
5. Ibid.
6. First Packer Confession, Alfred Packer Collection, Colorado State Archives. *Lake City Silver World*, March 24, 1883.
7. *Denver Republican,* March 17, 1883.
8. *Rocky Mountain News*, March 17, 1883.
9. Ibid.
10. The confession is taken from Second Packer Confession, Alfred Packer Collection, Colorado State Archives; *Rocky Mountain News*, *Denver Republican*, and *Denver Times*, March 17, 1883; *Lake City Silver World*, March 24, 1883; *The Case of Alfred*

Packer The Man-Eater: An Unsolved Mystery of the West by Paul H. Gantt, pp. 55-57; and *Alfred Packer: The True Story of the Man-Eater* by Robert W. "Red" Fenwick, pp. 17-19. Paragraph indentions are arranged for easier reading.

11. *Denver Republican*, March 17, 1883.

12. *Rocky Mountain News*, March 17, 1883.

13. *Saguache Chronicle*, March 23, 1883.

14. *Denver Republican*, March 17, 1883.

15. *Lake City Silver World*, April 14, 1883.

16. Ibid. Unless otherwise noted, all testimony comes from the *Lake City Silver World*, April 14, 1883.

17. *Lake City Silver World*, April 14, April 21, 1883. The Packer statement was reprinted in the latter edition.

18. Ibid.

19. Ibid.

20. Judge Gerry's Death Sentence of Packer, Hinsdale District Court Case #1883DC379, Alfred Packer Collection, Colorado State Archives; Gantt; Fenwick; *Rocky Mountain News*, *Lake City Silver World*, April 14, 1883.

21. *Rocky Mountain News*, August 6, 1886.

22. Ibid.

23. *Denver Sunday Times*, February 18, 1900.

24. *Denver Post*, April 26, 1907.

25. *Rocky Mountain News*, April 27, 1907.

26. *Littleton Independent*, April 26, 1907.

Chapter Seven

"You will never reach home alive"

Trial of Oliver Lee and James Gililland

‹‹———————————————————————————————››

Hillsboro, New Mexico Territory, 1899

Prelude

"Has Colonel A J Fountain been murdered?" the *El Paso Daily Herald* asked in its February 4, 1896, editions. The answer was obvious, especially since the article's headline proclaimed: COL. FOUNTAIN KILLED.[1] Yet more than a century later, the disappearance of Colonel Albert Jennings Fountain and his nine-year-old son, Henry,[2] remains one of the greatest mysteries in not only New Mexico, but the West.

For years southern New Mexico had attracted an assortment of hardcases, adventurers, ne'er-do-wells, rustlers, murderers, and thieves, a virtual who's who of westerners whose reputations often smelled like a week-old coyote carcass — Billy the Kid, Jessie Evans, Henry Brown, Lawrence Murphy, John Chisum, William Brady, James Dolan, John Slaughter, Pat Garrett, Bill McNew, James Gililland, and Oliver Lee. Men could build empires — in politics, cattle, or both — in violent Lincoln, Otero, and Doña Ana Counties. They could also make powerful enemies.

It was a land of opportunity.

Albert Jennings Fountain was one of many who came to New Mexico during this turbulent time. His background remains cloudy today. The *El Paso Daily Herald* gave this biographical sketch:

Col. Fountain was born 'in New York in 1838. He was educated at Columbia college. In his early youth he went to California, engaged in literary work, studied advocacy, enlisted in the first California volunteers in 1861, marched from the Pacific to the Rio Grande, served in New Mexico and Texas during the war and was promoted to lieutenant and captain. In 1865 he settled in El Paso, Texas. He was elected in 1866 as surveyor of the Bexar district, served in many civil positions and was elected to the state senate in 1868, serving until 1874. He received an appointment from Gov. Davis as brigadier general of the state guard in western Texas. In 1875 he moved to Mesilla, and soon had a large law practice.

Col. Fountain organized and was commissioned captain of Mesilla scouts in 1879. He took the field against Victoria, and was appointed major of cavalry in 1881, and in 1883 was ordered by Gov. Sheldon to suppress lawlessness in southern New Mexico. This work was effectively done in two months. A number of the rustlers were killed and many others were sent to the penitentiary. For this work he was presented with a service of silver plate by the citizens of Dona Ana county. He was made colonel of First New Mexico cavalry, and with this regiment he took the field against Geronimo in 1885. In 1885 he was elected to the legislature and was made speaker of the house of representatives. Later Col. Fountain was appointed special counsel for the government by President Cleveland and was appointed district attorney by President Harrison. He afterwards became counsel for the New Mexico Stock association and held that position at the time of his death.[3]

Although there is no record of him at Columbia College, he picked up an excellent education somewhere during his many travels. What else is known about him? He reportedly was born Albert Jennings. Why he took the surname Fountain has been debated over the years. In any event, he was a Mason, a staunch Republican, and as chief attorney and prosecutor for the Southeastern New Mexico Stock Growers Association, was working on eliminating the rustling problem in the territory.

Working against Jennings was another powerful attorney. Albert Bacon Fall was born in Frankfort, Kentucky, on November 26, 1861. His father served with Confederate cavalry genius Nathan Bedford Forrest and taught school after the war. Albert Fall, however, received little education and was working in a Nashville, Tennessee, cotton mill by the time he was eleven. In his teens, he moved west and indulged in a number of enterprises: cowboying, clerking, and mining. When his wife, Emma, received a diagnosis of tuberculosis around 1887, the Falls decided to settle in Las Cruces, New Mexico, where he dabbled in real estate and politics — he was a diehard Democrat — while practicing law.

Polar opposites, Fountain and Fall clashed. Fountain had established the Republican *Valley Independent* in Mesilla in 1877. Fall started the *Independent Democrat* in Las Cruces in 1892. In 1888 Fountain defeated Fall in the election for a seat in the New Mexico House of Representatives, but Fall still

The disappearance of Colonel Albert Jennings Fountain, along with his
young son, remains one of New Mexico's great mysteries.
(University of Texas at El Paso Library Special Collections Department)

became a political power in the territory. There were other thorns, best explained by noted historian Leon C. Metz in his biography of Pat Garrett: "Fall was a southerner; Fountain a Yankee.... Fall was young, ambitious, and power-hungry; Fountain middle-aged, ambitious, and already a political power. Fall sought to topple his adversary from his high position; Fountain struggled to hang on."[4]

In 1889 Fall struck up a friendship with rancher Oliver Milton Lee, who owned a large ranch near Dog Canyon in the Sacramento Mountains. Lee needed a good lawyer and a powerful political ally. Fall filled both bills.

Born in Buffalo Gap, Texas, on November 8, 1865, Lee had settled in the Tularosa Basin in 1884. He had a reputation as a gunman, and it wasn't long before he was suspected of killing Walter Good, whose body was found in the White Sands, a vast deposit of gypsum seventeen miles southwest of Alamogordo (home of White Sands National Monument today), in 1888 after feuding with Lee. In 1894 Lee became a prime suspect in the murder of Francois "Frenchy" Jean Rochas. He was never tried in either case, though. He worked alongside other gunmen, most prominently Texans William "Bill" McNew and James "Jim" Gililland. With that kind of reputation and associates, it came as little surprise that Lee was suspected of rustling in New Mexico. After all, rustling indictments were waiting for him back in Texas.

When the Southeastern New Mexico Stock Growers Association formed in March 1894, Lee joined, but when Fountain became the association's lawyer and started prosecuting rustlers, the transplanted Texan began worrying. Wanting to bring down Lee, Fountain began investigating the rise of Lee's herd and the increased rustling of his neighbors'. Of course,

Oliver Lee became a powerful rancher and state senator despite his association with Albert Fountain's disappearance. (University of Texas at El Paso Library Special Collections Department)

the downfall of Oliver Lee would certainly hurt the political future of his close friend, Albert Fall.

Fountain's case grew stronger, and on January 12, 1896, he left Mesilla for the grand jury convening in Lincoln. Fountain knew his life was in danger, but his wife, Mariana, persuaded him to take his youngest son, Henry, with him. Apparently, Mariana thought having Henry along would offer the prosecutor protection from assassins. After all, who would murder a nine-year-old boy?

Fountain's case came together nicely, and the grand jury returned thirty-two bills of indictment, including Cause Number 1489, which charged William McNew and Oliver Lee with larceny of cattle, and Cause Number 1890, which charged the two men with defacing brands. As Fountain left the Lincoln County Courthouse he was handed a note, which read: "If you drop this we will be your friends. If you go on with it you will never reach home alive."[5]

The threat did not stop the attorney. Fountain left for home with Henry on Thursday, January 30, stopping for the night at the home of Doctor J. H. Blazer eighteen miles away near Mescalero. The next morning he left for La Luz, nine miles south of Tularosa. Along the way he noticed two men on horseback trailing him. Concerned, he pushed his team pulling the buggy faster. On a wintry Saturday, February 1, the Fountains continued, reaching the edge of the White Sands around noon, where the man and boy ate lunch. By now, three men were following the buggy or riding directly ahead, always keeping far enough from the Fountains to avoid recognition. A few hours later on the road, the Fountains met up with mail carrier Santos Alvarado of Tularosa, talked a bit, and went their separate ways, the Fountains traveling past

Detail of New Mexico from an 1891 map shows the area of
Oliver Lee and Albert Jennings Fountain. (Author's Collection)

Luna's Well and into the San Andres foothills toward San
Agustin Pass.

A few miles east of Chalk Hill, the Fountains ran into
another mail carrier, Saturnino Barela of Las Cruces, one of
the colonel's good friends. Fountain, who was cradling a Winchester rifle on his lap, told Barela about the men following
him and his concerns. As the mail carrier told the *El Paso Daily
Herald*:

"I met Colonel Fountain near Chalk Hills, some forty miles from Las Cruces. Just before meeting him I saw three men on horseback, who seemed not to want to meet me and took across the plains at my approach. When I met Colonel Fountain he asked me if I knew who the horsemen were. I told him I did not and he then said they had been following or riding directly ahead of him for some time. He was suspicious of them.

"I told the Colonel that it would be best to come back to a neighboring ranch with me and that we would start to Las Cruces together Sunday morning. He studied the matter a moment, and then said: 'No, I will drive on. Good bye.' With this Colonel Fountain drove off, and I continued on my way."[6]

That Sunday Barela arrived in Mesilla and went straight to the Fountain house, asking Mariana if her husband and son had arrived safely. She fainted. Fountain and Henry had not reached home.

About five miles east of where he had met the colonel Saturday, Barela explained, he had come across signs where the colonel's wagon had left the road. Suspicious, he followed the tracks a while and saw prints from three horses trailing the buggy. Two of Fountain's sons (he had twelve children) quickly organized a search party.

The men returned Monday afternoon without Fountain and little Henry, dead or alive. They had found Fountain's wagon ten miles off the road. "The horses were gone," Barela said, "as was also the feed, the Colonel's rifle, and other articles which he had in the wagon. A box under the wagon seat, in which Colonel Fountain kept his papers, had been pulled out and the contents of the box were rumpled up as if having been gone through hurriedly. All around where the wagon was found could be traced the hoof prints of three horses."[7]

Jack Fountain added:

> We struck father's trail where he left the road and followed it to where he had evidently made a stop, and where from all indications he was taken prisoner by the men who were following him. The tracks show that horsemen approached him from three sides, and I think that owing to the presence of my little brother, father must have surrendered rather than have the little boy hurt.
>
> From there we followed the trails of the entire party to where we found the wagon. The foot-prints of both father and brother could be seen around the wagon.[8]

Later discoveries foretold of murder: cigarette papers, horse apples, and hoof prints in a bend in the road where men had obviously waited a long time; a knee print, footprint, and two empty rifle cartridges behind bushes near the road; a pool of dried blood and signs nearby where a blanket had been laid on the ground and something heavy put on top of it.

The searchers continued. East of where they found the abandoned buggy, they discovered a campsite where three men had cooked a meal, fed their horses, and laid something heavy on a blanket. The trail divided near the Sacramento Mountains. One horseman took off toward a lineshack at Wildy Well, so the posse split up. Several returned to Las Cruces and Mesilla with the colonel's wagon. Major W. H. H. Llewellyn took one group toward Oliver Lee's Dog Canyon ranch house but lost the trail when a group of Lee's cowboys drove a herd over it. Fountain's son-in-law, Carl Clausen, and a friend named Luis Herrera went after the lone rider. Finding Lee and three other men at Wildy Well, Clausen asked if Lee would help them look for Fountain and Henry. Lee shot back: "No, I haven't time. And that ____ is nothing to us."[9] Lee rode off, and Clausen examined the hoof prints. They were the same as the ones he had been trailing, so he and Herrera rode back to Mesilla to report the findings and suspicions.

Rewards and rumors shot up across New Mexico Territory. Albert Fountain was dead, and the prime suspects were obvious: Oliver Lee and Bill McNew (Albert Bacon Fall was also suspected). Or Albert Fountain had run off to start a new life and escape his wife. Few people believed the latter, but proving the first would be difficult with the politics of the time and a corrupt Doña Ana County sheriff's department. So Fountain's allies brought in Pat Garrett.

Famous for the slaying of Billy the Kid in 1881 when he was sheriff of Lincoln County, Garrett was semi-retired and living in Uvalde, Texas. The man who tracked down Billy the Kid and basically ended the bloody Lincoln County War seemed the perfect man for the job. In El Paso a council offered Garrett a deputy sheriff's job in Las Cruces at $300 a month. As soon as possible, Garrett would take the sheriff's job.

Politics — and Lee and Fall — muddled things up. The Pinkertons came in to investigate but had little luck. In April down in El Paso, a spiritualist claimed that the ghost of Albert Fountain came to him and said he was killed by two Americans and two Mexicans three miles east of the White Sands.

When Numa Reymond resigned as Doña Ana County sheriff in April, Garrett replaced him. Garrett was a Democrat, but he was backed by Republicans, so when the elections were held, he ran as an Independent, won easily, and then registered as a Republican. Yet for the next few years, Garrett took his time building a case against Fountain's murderers.

In the spring of 1897, Garrett pressed Judge Frank Parker for bench warrants for the arrest of Lee, Gililland, McNew, and Bill Carr, whom Garrett said he could prove had murdered the Fountains. He somehow got the warrants and quickly arrested McNew and Carr without incident, and they were held in the Las Cruces jail without bail. He made no attempt, however, to bring in Lee and Gililland, who soon went into hiding.

Fall came to the defense of the jailed men, and in April 1898 a preliminary hearing was held. Fall argued that there was insufficient evidence to hold the two on the charges, but the court only half agreed. Bill Carr was set free; Bill McNew was remanded and held without bail. That summer, with the outbreak of the Spanish-American War, Albert Bacon Fall left New Mexico to fight in Cuba (he never made it overseas, however), and Garrett decided now was his best chance to go after Lee and Gililland.

On July 12 Garrett and his deputies discovered the two fugitives hiding on a rooftop at Wildy Well. It was a fiasco for the new Doña Ana County sheriff and legendary lawman. In a gunbattle, deputy Kent Kearney was shot in the shoulder and groin, and a standoff ensued. Although the posse outnumbered Lee and Gililland, the latter two had the upper hand. Garrett asked Lee to surrender. Lee refused and reminded Garrett of his own predicament. A truce was called, allowing the posse to leave their guns on the ground and take off with their tails between their legs. An embarrassed Garrett asked a section crew to fetch Kearney, who died of his wounds the following day. Lee and Gililland escaped again.

By the time Fall returned, Lee and Gililland had another charge over them — the murder of Deputy Sheriff Kent Kearney. Fall realized he had to move fast. The two men couldn't hide out forever, and now Garrett would be gunning for them. The wily attorney soon negotiated surrender terms for his two clients. Lee and Gililland would not be Garrett's prisoners, nor would they be held in the Doña Ana County jail. The two men surrendered without incident in March.

Now the prosecution and Fall had to prepare for a trial. Bill McNew would be tried separately from Lee and Gililland, and the prosecution decided to go after Lee and Gililland instead, fearing that if McNew were tried first, Albert Fall would be able to prepare a better defense. The territory would not prosecute McNew, and the murder indictments against Lee and Gililland for the deaths of Albert Fountain and Kent Kearney were put aside for now. Instead, Lee and Gililland would be tried for the murder of little Henry Fountain. But where? Otero County — Lee's base — was out. So was Las Cruces and Mesilla, home of Fountain. So a trial date of May 25, 1899 — three years after Fountain and his son disappeared — was set in Hillsboro, Sierra County.

Trial

A mining town in the Black Range, Hillsboro came about with the discovery of gold in 1877. Despite frequent Apache raids, the town boomed and prospered, boasting a newspaper, several saloons, public school, and in 1892 the brick- and stone-trimmed Sierra County Courthouse. On the other hand, even by 1899 the town lacked telephones and a telegraph line and had no railroad spur to connect the town of two hundred to the rest of New Mexico. With a horde of regional and national journalists converging on the town, Western Union strung a telegraph wire from Hillsboro to Lake Valley, the nearest railroad station, and sent a telegraph operator, B. R. Brooks, son of the company manager in El Paso, to Hillsboro.

Site of another "trial of the century": Sierra County Courthouse in Hillsboro, New Mexico. This photo was taken circa 1895-1905 by George T. Miller. (Courtesy, Museum of New Mexico, Negative Number 76553)

"For the first time in the history of Hillsboro the busy click, click of the telegraph instrument connected with a wire that stretches across the mountains and valleys and unites, twenty miles away, with a myriad of other wires that lead to all parts of the United States and the world," the *El Paso Daily Herald* reported.[10]

From Lake Valley people rode the stage and swarmed into the county seat to watch what was becoming the trial of the century.

The Union Hotel didn't have enough rooms, and the prosecution and defense planned on calling seventy-five witnesses. The problem was solved with the creation of tent cities, separate camps for the defense and prosecution. Since this was shaping up to be a Republican-versus-Democrat, Yankee-versus-Rebel trial, it's little wonder that the territory's witnesses set up camp, complete with guards, north of Hillsboro while the defense team pitched tents in what was called the Oliver Lee Camp, complete with a chuck wagon, south of town.

The situation was tense.

Tonight [Hillsboro] is overcrowded with notables from all parts of southern New Mexico and feeling over the case on trial is great and the deadliest enmity exists between some of the staunch friends of Lee and Gililland, and as they are constantly brushing one another's elbows on the sidewalks an outbreak may occur at any moment. The tension is great and a sort of ominous silence pervades the town, like a calm before a storm. Groups of interested persons are to be seen earnestly discussing the details of the situation in low tones. The tall form of Pat Garrett appeared late this evening as the slayer of "Billy the Kid" wended his way along the sidewalks. Near him stood Judge A. B. Fall, Captain Curry, William McNew and others conversing.[11]

Prosecuting the two defendants were District Attorney R. P. Barnes of Silver City, William Burr Childers of Albuquerque, hired by the Masons, and Thomas Benton Catron of Santa Fe, the latter appointed as special counsel by Governor Miguel Otero. Catron was a fine lawyer and great speaker, but he had long been associated with the notorious Santa Fe Ring, synonymous for power and corruption. Assisting Bacon for the defense were Harvey B. Fergusson of Albuquerque and Harry M. Daugherty of Socorro.

On May 25 the prosecution asked for a continuance so more witnesses could arrive. Fifteen had failed to appear. One witness from North Dakota had a change of heart, or nerve, and did not show. Three Mexican cowboys, who allegedly had seen three men ride off with the bodies of Albert and Henry Fountain strapped to horses, lit a shuck for Mexico. That left the prosecution depending on Jack Maxwell of Three Rivers, and he was missing. Garrett took a posse in search for Maxwell.

Maxwell was a bit of a gamble for the prosecution anyway. "He was the principal witness at the preliminary hearing of Billy McNew, but proved to be a good deal of a boomerang to the territory, as he contradicted himself on many important and material points. His testimony, however, was damaging to the defense, and his manner led many to believe that he was holding something back, and knows a great deal more than he would tell. Friends of the prosecution declared their belief that he was being intimidated by friends of the defendants. The defendants and their friends, on the other hand, profess to ridicule the idea and boldly declare that his whole testimony was a pure fabrication."[12]

Things didn't improve for the prosecution. William Childers began to complain that the Masons hadn't paid him for his services, and it took a collection drive in Las Cruces to stop his bellyaching.

It took three days for a jury to be seated. As many of the jurors spoke only Spanish, an interpreter was hired. Witnesses began taking the stand on Monday, May 29.

William T. "Poker Bill" Thornton, former governor of New Mexico, testified first. He had taken the train to Las Cruces upon hearing of the Fountains' disappearance, and he took blood-soaked sand, found near the abandoned wagon, and blood-stained hair from Fountain's white horse, which he gave to a Santa Fe chemist. The chemist ruled the blood was human.

Antonia Garcia, wife of Albert Fountain Junior, followed, and her husband took the stand after her. Both told of the discovery of the abandoned buggy and the trailing of the tracks to within seven miles of Lee's ranch in Dog Canyon. Saturnino Barela recalled his last conversation with Colonel Fountain.

Next up was Theodore Heman, who had served as foreman of the grand jury that indicted Lee and McNew. Heman swore that Fountain had been responsible for those indictments. Fall vehemently objected, but Judge Parker overruled him.

Meanwhile, Jack Maxwell had been found — captured might be a better word — in White Oaks or Alamogordo (George Curry, Pat Garrett, and deputies named Latham and Williams have been given the credit by myriad sources) and was taken to Hillsboro. On the stand, Maxwell said he had spent the night of February 1, 1896, at Lee's ranch and saw four men ride in the next morning. He recognized three of them — Lee, Gililland, and McNew. However Maxwell's memory was faulty, and transcripts from his preliminary hearing testimony had to be read back to him — over objections from the defense. Fall slammed Maxwell in cross-examination, bringing out his aliases while living in Alabama, Texas, and

Colorado, hammering on Maxwell's terrible memory about dates, and accusing Maxwell of having told Garrett he wouldn't testify unless he was paid $2,000. Maxwell denied this.

Cowboy James Gould next said Gililland had arrived at McNew's house on the night before the disappearances and picked up some cartridges. Gililland also said to tell anyone asking that he was going to Roswell, only he rode north toward Dog Canyon.

> "Later I had a talk with Gililland, and he said Col. Fountain (applying a vile name) came from Texas in a chicken coop."

Said the witness: "Gilliland said the deceased raised up hades everywhere he went, but would not do so again. I remarked he might have needed killing, but not his son. Gilliland then said the boy was a half-breed and it was no more than killing a dog."[13]

Under cross-examination, the defense got Gould, a cousin of Gililland's wife, to admit that he was an enemy of Gililland and McNew. Fall also asked the witness where he was in March 1897. Gould answered that he had been in jail.

Riley Baker, a former deputy sheriff and Gililland's brother-in-law, said Gililland once pointed out where he, McNew, and Lee watched the Fountains with telescopes or binoculars. "When I deprecated the killing of the child, Gililland said he thought it (the child) little better than a dog.... He said if the bodies of Col. Fountain and son had to be found before any one was convicted no one would be convicted. Later he said things had been more quiet since old Fountain's disappearance."[14]

Like Oliver Miller, James Gililland had a reputation as a hard gunman.
Many believe he slit young Henry Fountain's throat.
(University of Texas at El Paso Library Special Collections Department)

Another cowboy, Frank Wayne, said Lee cautioned him
after the disappearances not to say that he had seen Lee riding toward Dog Canyon "as it might interfere with his [Lee's]
plans."[15]

Albert Fall had raised reasonable doubt with his hard
questioning on cross-examination, bringing out points that the
witnesses had reason to lie, were, in fact, enemies of the
defendants, or had shady backgrounds. Now the prosecution

needed a strong witness to salvage its case. Pat Garrett took the stand.

The *Rio Grande Republican* of Las Cruces summarized Garrett's testimony for the territory:

"I found blood where we supposed the murder of Col. Fountain took place. I was accompanied by a posse. The bloody spot indicated at once a murder had been done. The ground was soaked and the blood had spurted. A few feet away there was another small spot of blood. In April of 1898, I went to serve a warrant on Lee and Gilliland and they objected and killed one of my men. I had made several efforts to arrest them, even going to Lee's camp and cow herd but failed to find them. When they killed my deputy we went into Lee's house and searched the rooms but failed to find Lee and Gilliland. After looking outside I found a ladder sticking out from the roof and McVey, who lived at Lee's house was out in the yard making signs toward the roof. I sent a man up on the shed and he saw an arm protruding. I told Matteson, another of Lee's friends to tell him [Lee] we had a warrant for him and to come down. He said if Lee was there he didn't know it. All he could do was to crawl after them. We ordered their hands up without effect. H. K. Kearney, one of my men, fired after he had crawled-up. Lee then fired. Kearney was mortally wounded, dying a short time afterwards and there was quite a fusilade [sic] around us."

Skipping subsequent events the witness told of the voluntary surrender of Lee and Gilliland several weeks later. Regarding the sensational contract referred to yesterday by the defense, Garrett told of the written contract with Jack Maxwell, which he last saw in Mrs. Creed's safe on the VV ranch. "I have a correct copy here, made by myself," he said. The contract reads as follows.

Tularosa, N.M., March 6 1898.

This is to certify that we, the undersigned, agree to pay John Maxwell two thousand dollars, in case he gives us information that will lead to the arrest and conviction of the murderers of Col. A. J. Fountain and son, said money to be due as soon as conviction is had.

P. F. GARRETT.

Garrett's testimony continued on June 2, when Fall got his chance on cross. Fall had been masterful in attacking other prosecution witnesses, but Pat Garrett proved to be a handful.

Q. What was the condition of affairs when you went to Cruces?

A. You fellows had been shooting at one another and cutting up.

Q. What fellows?

A. You, Lee, Williams and, others.

Q. With the present evidence in your possession why did you wait two years to procure warrants for the defendants.

A. You had too much control of the courts down there. (laughter).

Q. In other words, you waited for a change in administration and you thought I was the administration.

A. You came pretty near being it.[16]

Garrett had more than held his own, but other witnesses lacked his prowess.

The Santa Fe chemist employed by then-Governor Thornton took the stand to say the blood he found was human. On cross-examination, however, Professor Francis Crossen admitted he only thought the blood was human, that he couldn't tell for sure without a microscope and that he had not used one during his examination. "He broke down completely under the rapid fire of questions by Attorney Fall..."[17] John Meadows, who found the blood, didn't fare much better under Fall's cross when he was forced to admit that he had ridden with Billy the Kid in Texas and once associated with other outlaws. "He claimed to be a victim of circumstances in each case."[18]

On June 3 Captain Thomas Brannigan, a scout, gave convincing circumstantial evidence of his discoveries during the search for the Fountains. Brannigan

"told that there were evidences of a party having carried a heavy object on a horse and deposited it on a blanket at night. This was given foundation yesterday by the evidence of the trail of a bloody blanket. The tracks of a child's shoe were light and only of one foot and two or four feet apart, as if they had been made with a shoe on the hand.

"I measured the tracks of three men about the bloody camp at other camps along the trail of seven horses from this point," said the witness, "and the next day found tracks on Lee's dirt roof exactly like the one having a heel run over that I found in the camps. I preserved the measurements. When McNew, who was originally charged with complicity, came to Las Cruces, a short time later, I waited for a chance and measured his tracks; these gave the same measurement as the others about the camps. The tracks of Lee's horses also corresponded with three of the largest horses on the trail from the bloody camp."[19]

Brannigan also held his ground under Fall's relentless cross. Other witnesses including Fountain's friend Major W. H. H. Llewellyn took the stand for the prosecution, offering more circumstantial evidence that pointed to Oliver Lee. Meanwhile, a group of Hillsboro women sent flowers to the defendants, and the bouquet was placed on the defense table. "The Oliver Lee Trial and telegraph communications with the outside world furnishes as much excitement as Hillsboro can stand just at this time," the *El Paso Times* commented.[20]

With the case going against them, Barnes, Catron, and Childers took exception to media coverage and issued a notice published in many newspapers: "All newspaper reports, including Associated Press, sent from here about trial of Lee and Gililland are gross misrepresentations of evidence and facts generally. We ask you to publish this daily until trial is over or we notify you that misrepresentations have ceased."[21]

After the prosecution closed with a whimper on June 6, the defense asked the judge to instruct the jury to find a verdict of not guilty and end the trial. Judge Parker denied the motion, and court was adjourned until June 7, when the defense began its phase.

George Curry said Jack Maxwell had told him Lee, Gililland, and McNew were at the ranch when the Fountains disappeared. Curry also said that, as special agent appointed by Governor Otero, he had obtained a confession from "Slick" Miller that said Miller and two others were behind the Fountain and three other murders. The prosecution objected to this, and Parker sustained the motion. Under cross-examination, Curry admitted his indebtedness to Oliver Lee.

Bud Smith also said Maxwell told him the three suspects had been at the ranch, and Joe Morgan, "a wealthy stock grower," said he saw the defendants at the ranch on the day of the alleged murder. Albert Blevins, a fireman for the Texas and Pacific Railway, helped strengthen the alibi when he testified that the defendants were at the ranch. "The witness said the cattle, which the prosecution claimed to have been used to obliterate the trails, were under contract to be delivered and that Lee was with him the day he met the herd.... The prosecution held the witness nearly three hours, vainly trying to confuse him."[22]

The defense grew so confident, half its witnesses were released without being called to the stand.

Lee's mother also gave her son an alibi. No surprise there.

And so things went.

Oliver Lee took the stand in his own defense, saying he didn't know of the murders until several days later. The fear of being killed by a mob kept him in hiding, he said.

The last defense witness was Print Rhode, Lee's brother-in-law, who "had a bombshell" when he "implicated Major Llewellyn in a plot to assassinate Lee by blowing up his house" with dynamite. "The spectators almost broke forth in cheers. The sympathy of the local community, particularly the ladies, is now with the defendants."[23]

The defense rested. James Gililland never took the stand.

To rebut Rhode's testimony, the prosecution brought forth a number of witnesses, including Brannigan and Carl Clausen. Major Llewellyn made no such threat, they swore.

Final arguments were delivered Saturday and Monday, eighteen days after the trial began. Barnes and Childers spoke first for the prosecution with Childers telling the jury no body had to be produced for a guilty verdict. In defense closings, Fergusson charged Catron with deliberately lying during his examinations, and Fall called Jack Maxwell a liar. Other witnesses for the territory had reasons to lie. "You would not hang a yellow dog on the evidence presented here," Fall said, "not less two men."[24]

Catron made the final appeal in a two-and-one-half-hour speech that began at eight Monday night. Parker then charged the jurors and said they could retire for the evening, but a short while later the defense objected, and Parker recalled the jury. After deliberating only seven minutes, the jury announced its decision at midnight.

Not guilty.

"A murmer [sic] of applause swept over the court room when the announcement was made and the defendants and their attorneys...were warmly congratulated," the *El Paso Daily Herald* reported.[25]

Handshakes all around on the defense table. Meanwhile, newspaper correspondent J.H. McCutcheon was then taken into custody for contempt of court. He had irked the prosecution with his trial coverage, but he was released a short time later on his own recognizance.

The trial of the century was over, but the mystery had not been solved.

Aftermath

Oliver Lee and James Gililland were immediately transferred to Alamogordo via El Paso to await a September trial in Silver City for the killing of Kent Kearney. At El Paso, Lee told a reporter: "I anticipate no trouble at Alamogordo. My friends will give the authorities no trouble. We will wait for trial in jail if we can not get out on bail. Our hope is to secure bail through habeas corpus proceedings if Judge Parker does not conclude to release us without an order. In any event, however, there will be no violence as has been reported."[26]

There wasn't. Neither Lee, Gililland, nor McNew were ever prosecuted. All charges were eventually dropped. The jury had spoken, but were the men really innocent?

"It has always been hard for me to believe that Oliver Lee could have had anything to have done with the murder," H. F. Chaves of Las Cruces recalled in 1938, "but for the other men they were the type — gunmen that lived the life of out-laws."[27]

Others weren't so sure. In fact many believed Lee and Gililland had gotten away with murder. They probably had.

In October 1900 James Canyon discovered two skulls and some bones about five miles from Cloudcroft. At first it was believed that the bones were the remains of Colonel Fountain and Henry, but that was later disproved, and the mystery continued.

In 1950, according to the *El Paso Times*, an unidentified man made a deathbed confession that he had taken part in the murders and allegedly produced a Masonic Lodge pen Fountain was believed to have been wearing when he vanished. According to this man, he and two other men — dead by 1950 — ambushed Fountain, mortally wounded him, and took the colonel, his son, and the wagon through the White Sands, knowing the wind-swept gypsum would wipe out the trail, and then drew straws to see who would kill Henry. The loser cut the boy's throat, and the body was dumped in an alkaline pit. The boy's father was buried in a canyon in the San Andres Mountains.

Searchers pored over the spot identified by the man, but no body was found. The mystery continued.

Historian Leon C. Metz uncovered a similar story he published in his outstanding biography *Pat Garrett: The Story of a Western Lawman*. In 1969 an old cowboy named Butler Oral "Snooks" Burris, who had known James Gililland, told Metz that Gililland often said, while drunk, that he had taken part in the killings and had no regrets over murdering the colonel but cried when recalling young Henry's brutal death. Gililland drew straws with Lee and McNew, and Gililland lost, drew his knife, and slit Henry's throat.

Still, the bodies were never found, so the mystery remained unsolved, and all parties died off, never saying for the record what happened in 1894 in the White Sands. Pat Garrett was murdered in 1908, not far from where the Fountains vanished. Bill McNew died in 1937, James Gililland in 1946. Oliver Lee, who became a major cattleman and served two terms in the state senate in the 1920s, died in 1941. His legacy endures at a state park named after him south of Alamogordo. Powerful Albert Bacon Fall's fame rose, and he was appointed secretary of the interior during President Harding's administration only to be brought down in disgrace during the Teapot Dome scandal. He died in 1944.

As far as the Hillsboro verdict is concerned, perhaps the *New Mexican* put it best:

> Brushing aside all other controversies in the recent murder trial at Hillsboro, a sufficient explanation for the acquittal of the defendants is that the death of the boy they were accused of murdering could not be proved by the prosecution. There was no witness to the crime, the body was not discovered, not any produced who could swear of his own knowledge that the

boy is not alive. Of course, no one believes that either father or son were spared by cattle thieves, but as yet this has been shown only by circumstances or presumption though it is presumption of the very strongest sort, so strong that it amounts in a moral certainty. In addition to this lack of positive evidence, the defense relied upon an alibi to establish a claim that they could not have committed the crime at the time of the disappearance of the two persons. It is to be hoped that the prosecution can yet find a witness to the death of the victims. Then the truth or falsity of the alibi testimony will be of more importance in the trial of the same men upon a charge of murdering Colonel Fountain. Public opinion as to the guilt or innocence of these defendants has not been materially changed by the recent trial.[28]

It has been said that Oliver Lee, Bill McNew, and James Gililland committed the perfect murder. Maybe someday someone will come across the bones of a man and a small boy. Maybe DNA testing and other twenty-first-century technology will lead to a beyond-a-reasonable-doubt conclusion regarding the fate of Albert Jennings Fountain and Henry Fountain — and their murderers.

Until then, the mystery endures.

Chapter Notes

Primary sources: *The Life and Death of Colonel Albert Jennings Fountain* (University of Oklahoma Press, 1965) by A. M. Gibson; *Pat Garrett: The Story of a Western Lawman* (University of Oklahoma Press, 1974) by Leon C. Metz; *Tularosa: Last of the Frontier West*

(University of New Mexico Press, 1960, 1980) by C. L. Sonnichsen; and various 1896-99 editions of the *Albuquerque Daily Citizen, El Paso Daily Herald, El Paso Times, Rio Grande Republican,* and *Santa Fe Daily New Mexican.*

1. *El Paso Daily Herald,* February 4, 1896.

2. Henry's reported age at the time of his disappearance ranges from six to nine, but most historians cite the correct age as nine.

3. Ibid.

4. Metz, Leon C. *Pat Garrett: The Story of a Western Lawman,* p. 167.

5. Sonnichsen, C. L. *Tularosa: Last of the Frontier West,* p. 117.

6. *El Paso Daily Herald,* February 4, 1896.

7. Ibid.

8. Ibid.

9. *Tularosa,* p. 130.

10. *El Paso Daily Herald,* May 27, 1899.

11. Ibid.

12. *El Paso Times* quoted in the *Santa Fe Daily New Mexican,* May 29, 1899.

13. *Albuquerque Daily Citizen,* June 1, 1899.

14. Ibid.

15. *Rio Grande Republican,* June 2, 1899.

16. *El Paso Daily Herald,* June 2, 1899.

17. *Albuquerque Daily Citizen,* June 3, 1899.

18. Ibid.

19. Ibid.

20. *El Paso Times,* June 3, 1899.

21. *Albuquerque Daily Citizen,* June 9, 1899.

22. *Albuquerque Daily Citizen,* June 8, 1899.

23. *Albuquerque Daily Citizen,* June 10, 1899.

24. *El Paso Daily Herald*, June 15, 1899.

25. *El Paso Daily Herald*, June 13, 1899.

26. *Santa Fe Daily New Mexican*, June 14, 1899.

27. H. F. Chaves memoir, 1938, WPA Writers' Project.

28. *Santa Fe Daily New Mexican*, June 15, 1899.

Chapter Eight

"Don't, Uncle Bill, this is Lynn"

Trial of Wiley Lynn

«———————————————————»

Wewoka, Oklahoma, 1925

Prelude

Sam Elliott played him, in the 1999 TNT movie *You Know My Name* (based on Matt Braun's novel), as a highly principled lawman who died tragically while fighting for justice in an Oklahoma hellhole, and most historians have agreed with that assessment over the years. In her 1998 book *Shoot from the Lip: The Lives, Legends and Lies of the Three Guardsmen of Oklahoma and U.S. Marshal Nix*, however, revisionist historian Nancy B. Samuelson shot Bill Tilghman's image full of holes, painting him as a self-promoting SOB who spent plenty of time on the other side of the law, including when wearing a badge, while his assailant, federal peace officer Wiley Lynn, albeit no saint, killed the Oklahoma legend in self-defense.

So who was Bill Tilghman? Did he die performing his duty despite being a senior citizen? Was justice carried out in Wewoka, Oklahoma, in 1925? To understand that, you must first examine the victim.

William Matthew Tilghman Jr. was born in Fort Dodge, Iowa, in 1854, the son of William M. Tilghman Sr., a veteran of the Civil Wars and Indian wars, and Amanda M. Shepherd.

Around 1868 the family, including older brother Richard, older sister Mary, younger brother Francis, or Frank, and younger sisters Josephine and Harriet, moved to Atchison County, Kansas. Still in his teens, Tilghman drifted west in the early 1870s — legendary lawman/gambler Bat Masterson described him as a "slim-built, bright-looking youth" — working several years on the frontier as a buffalo hunter. Samuelson, of course, is correct in that Tilghman didn't walk the straight and narrow all of his life; few frontier lawmen, from Wyatt Earp and Bill Hickok, to television's Matt Dillon for that matter, did. Even the *Dodge City Times* called Tilghman a "hard citizen."[1]

Tilghman joined up with Hurricane Bill Martin and Dutch Henry Born (or Borne) in the spring of 1874, stealing horses from Indians and selling the livestock in Dodge City, Kansas. Tilghman's older brother, Richard, was killed in Kansas about the time — some say by Indians, others by vigilantes — and Tilghman, by his own account, drifted to Colorado and Wyoming, but he was soon back in Kansas. He was part-owner of Dodge City's Crystal Palace Saloon and served briefly as a deputy under Sheriff Charlie Bassett, yet he found himself arrested in early 1878 and charged, along with hardcases Dave Rudabaugh and Edgar West, with attempted robbery in Kinsley, Kansas. The charge against Tilghman was soon dropped — he said he had been mistaken for a man named Tillman — but he was arrested again for horse stealing. Again, the charges were dropped. At some point in the mid-1870s, he married Flora Kendall.

Although Tilghman apparently had served as a Ford County sheriff's deputy, his legend as a lawman did not begin until 1884 when he pinned on a badge again after his appointment as Dodge City marshal. In that capacity,

Marshal Bill Tilghman, upholder of the law or tarnished badge?
(Western History Collections, University of Oklahoma Library)

Tilghman chased horse thieves, arrested drunks, and got into at least one shooting scrap with some cowboys. He also handled himself ably during several fires that swept through Dodge City, even hauling a ladder himself and helping move materials from the *Journal* offices at Chestnut Street and First Avenue in 1885. He may or may not have arrested "Mysterious Dave" Mather after the gunman killed an assistant marshal in 1884 (Mather was acquitted). His career as marshal seemed fairly uneventful — compared to Hickok's and Earp's legends — and he resigned in March 1886.

By then he had several business enterprises going, including ranching, but he used his guns and made a reputation during the County Seat Wars of the late 1880s. In 1887 the towns of Leoti and Coronado had been vying to become the county seat of Wichita County, and bloodshed became common. Tilghman may have been acting as a sheriff's deputy during the war and met up with Ed Prather on Independence Day 1888 in Farmer City. Prather and Tilghman had argued that day, and by all accounts the former was drunk and the latter cold sober. The final argument came in a saloon when Prather threatened to kill Tilghman, who drew his gun and shot Prather twice. Prather died, and Tilghman was never prosecuted.

A year later Tilghman took part in another County Seat War, this one between rival towns Cimarron and Ingalls in Gray County. When the votes showed that Cimarron had won, millionaire Asa T. Soule, an Ingalls backer, claimed election fraud and asked for a court order to stop certification. The order was granted, and the feud continued, culminating on January 12, 1889.

That's when a group of gunmen, hired by Soule, raided the Gray County Courthouse in Cimarron on a Sunday morning and stole court records. The gunmen included Tilghman and Bat Masterson's brother Jim. One Cimarron resident was killed in the ensuing fight.

Three months later Tilghman left Kansas for Oklahoma Territory, taking part in the land run on April 22, 1889. If Tilghman's career as a Kansas lawman had been shadowy at best, he earned a mostly stellar (though certainly not unchallenged) reputation in Oklahoma. He served as a lawman in Guthrie and Perry and then staked a claim around Chandler. In 1891 Tilghman was appointed deputy U.S. marshal. Deputy Marshals Chris Madsen and Heck Thomas would also serve under U.S. Marshal Ed Nix, and Madsen, Thomas, and Tilghman would become known as the Three Guardsmen of Oklahoma.

Oklahoma Territory of the 1890s was filled with plenty of hardcases on the owlhoot trail — men like Bill Dalton, Bill Doolin, Tulsa Jack Blake, Bitter Creek Newcomb, Red Buck Waightman, Arkansas Tom Jones, and Dynamite Dick Clifton — and the Guardsmen were assigned to bring them in, dead or alive. In 1896 Tilghman tracked down Bill Doolin at the health spa in Eureka Springs, Arkansas, capturing the outlaw by surprise single-handedly and bringing him back to Oklahoma, although Doolin escaped from the jail only to be shot dead by Thomas shortly thereafter.

In 1898 Tilghman arrested members of a mob that had lynched two young Indians who had been accused of raping and murdering a white woman. The Indians were innocent, and Tilghman helped send eight of the lynchers to prison. He also eventually captured the real rapist-murderer.

He was elected sheriff of Lincoln County in 1900, the same year his first wife (or at least common-law wife), Flora, died of tuberculosis. On July 16, 1903, Tilghman married Zoe

Agnes Stratton in Ingalls, Oklahoma. She was twenty-two; he was forty-nine.

The next year Tilghman decided not to run for re-election — possibly because of charges of corruption in the office — but remained deputy U.S. marshal. He ran again for sheriff in 1907 but lost to Lew Martin by 176 votes.

In 1910 he successfully campaigned for state senator but resigned in July 1911 to take the job as police chief of Oklahoma City, where he cracked down on bootleggers, gambling parlors, and prostitutes. He resigned in 1913 to concentrate on his campaign to earn the appointment as United States marshal for the Western District of Oklahoma, but he lost out to J. Q. Newell, who also beat out Tilghman for the job in 1917.

Now in his sixties and often called "Uncle Bill" or "Uncle Billy," Tilghman showed no signs of slowing down. Instead of chasing bad guys (or being a badman himself), Tilghman stepped behind the new moving picture cameras to make a film, *The Passing of the Oklahoma Outlaws*, in 1915.

"Bill" Tilghman, probably the best-known peace officer in Oklahoma, whose career in the early days of Oklahoma prior to statehood, reads like a romance, is in Guthrie today. Tonight he will lecture at the Highland theater in connection with the picture "Passing of the Oklahoma Outlaws." The picture is a true historic reproduction of the pioneer days of Oklahoma and shows many interesting scenes, in which famous outlaws such as Bill Doolin, Bill Dalton, Al Jennings and Henry Starr, are principal actors.

The picture is six reels long and is considered one of the very best ever thrown on the canvas. [E. D.] Nix, former United States marshal of Oklahoma:

Bill Tilghman was serving as Oklahoma City's police chief (1911-13) when he posed for this photo with fellow lawman Chris Madsen, left. (Archives & Manuscripts Division of the Oklahoma Historical Society, Photo Number 5608)

William Tilghman, Chris Madsen, Heck Thomas and Bud Ledbetter, all noted officers during the "wild days," appear in the picture also.

It is a wonderful and a thrilling picture and well worth the time of any one to witness. The usual prices prevail.[2]

The movie, however, wasn't as profitable as Tilghman hoped. His health wasn't the best (he reportedly had cancer), and he had three young sons and a wife and plenty of debt. In 1924, ignoring objections from his family and friends, seventy-year-old Bill Tilghman decided to pin on a badge one last time. He went to Cromwell.

In Seminole County northeast of Wewoka, Cromwell sprung up in October 1923 after oil was discovered on a nearby farm. Booming oil towns in the Roaring Twenties attracted all sorts, and Cromwell was no exception. In only months the population ballooned to an estimated eight thousand to ten thousand. Prohibition was the law, but gin joints were the norm. So were swindlers, prostitutes, thieves, murderers, and hijackers. Cromwell quickly earned the moniker of the "wickedest city in the world." People disappeared in the middle of the night, their bodies to be discovered later dumped in oil tanks.

The law-abiding faction asked the sheriff to appoint a special deputy, and when the sheriff refused, the town leaders appealed to Governor Martin E. Trapp. Trapp listened and appointed Tilghman his special agent. Or did he? On May 24, 1925, during the murder trial, Trapp said in Oklahoma City that, although he respected Tilghman, the lawman had no state authority during his tenure as Cromwell marshal.

Street scene of Cromwell, the "wickedest city in the world," from the 1920s.
(Courtesy, www.BillTilghman.org)

Whether or not he had Trapp's backing, Tilghman came to Cromwell as a peace officer.

"Mr. Tilghman took up his duties last Saturday afternoon and states that he expects to work with the sheriff's office in making Cromwell a safer and more desirable place to live in," reported the *Cromwell News*, which also labeled Tilghman "Oklahoma's most noted peace officer."[3]

Tilghman brought with him law officer Buck Stevenson of Oklahoma City. Two other lawmen in Cromwell were Sheriff J. A. "Blanch" Doyle and federal prohibition officer Wiley Lynn. Lynn is often portrayed as corrupt, in cahoots with bootleggers (*You Know My Name* depicted him as a drug addict and insane killer, but that's Hollywood for you), however, he was making arrests and destroying illegal booze. Although

Lynn had been a fed since only the spring, he had previously served as a sheriff's deputy in Marshall County, Oklahoma. A member of the Choctaw Nation with a tribal allotment, he was in his mid-thirties with a wife and teen-age son.

On the night of November 1, 1924, Tilghman met Lynn. Tilghman-backers say Lynn was angry that Tilghman refused to take a bribe or wouldn't look the other way when it came to bootleggers. Lynn was drunk, they say, when Tilghman tried to arrest him. On the other hand, the anti-Tilghman faction says that when Lynn arrived to raid "Pop" Murphy's dance hall in Cromwell, Tilghman tried to stop him.

At some point that night, Lynn arrived at Cromwell by automobile, traveling with a Fort Sill soldier named Sergeant David Thompson and two women, Eva Caton and Rose Lutke. When Lynn's pistol discharged, Tilghman came outside to investigate, and the two men grappled. Tilghman was shot two or three times and collapsed, and Lynn drove off to Holdenville, where he turned himself in to Hughes County Sheriff Sam Turner and U.S. Commissioner Park Crutcher.

Hit twice in his lung, Tilghman was taken to the used-furniture store next door to the dance hall. Twenty minutes later he was dead.

The *Ardmore Statesman* reported:

> On last Saturday, at Cromwell, the Ragtown in Seminole county that has held a prominent place in the news headlines for several months, Bill Tilghman, one of the best known peace officers in the state, was shot to death by Wylie Lynn, an enforcement officer, whose former home was in Marshall county, [and] who is well known in this city.
>
> When things got so bad in Cromwell that the local deputy sheriffs could not handle the situation, the

town was incorporated and the new officials looked about for a man for the job of city marshal. They selected "Bill" Tilghman, former chief of police of Oklahoma City, and peace officer of territorial days, who had sustained a reputation for many years as one of the very best law officers for a bad community, that has ever lived in the territory, and in the state of Oklahoma.

Last Saturday about night Wylie Lynn, who has been for several months an "enforcement officer" in Oklahoma, rode into Cromwell, accompanied by two women and a man, all of whom are said to have been very drunk. The...four had been riding around Seminole and Hughes county all the afternoon, and their condition had been noticed in all the places they passed [through]. Driving up to the sidewalk opposite the Murphy dance hall concerning which so much has appeared in the papers recently, Lynn stepped out of the Ford and, taking a pistol from his pocket, shot it off "just to see if it would go", he is said to have said. The shot called Tilghman out of the Murphy place, accompanied by a friend. Meeting Lynn on the sidewalk he ordered him to give up the gun, and submit to arrest. Lynn replied by a move to [shoot], but Tilghman caught his hand and, with the assistance of his friend, took the gun from Lynn, who dropped his hand in his pocket and drew another gun, with which he shot Tilghman three times. Tilghman kept hold of Lynn until the second gun was taken from him, then crumpled to the sidewalk, mortally wounded....

The entire state, was shocked by this tragedy. Tilghman was known and liked all over the state, and is sincerely mourned. He was over 70 years of age at the time Lynn killed him.[4]

Tilghman's body lay in state at the capitol before he was buried at Oak Park Cemetery in Chandler. Governor Trapp, former Governor J. B. Robertson, former Tilghman deputies William Crume, G. M. Swanson, General Roy Hoffman, and U.S. Marshal Alva McDonald reportedly were chosen to serve as pallbearers. Tilghman left no will, so his estate was divided between his wife and six children. As Tilghman's friends and family, and indeed much of Oklahoma, mourned the lawman's passing, the state prepared to prosecute federal agent Wiley Lynn on a charge of murder.

Trial

For months after Tilghman's death, state and federal officers battled in court for the right to try Wiley Lynn. The state argued that prosecuting under Oklahoma law would be more direct; federal authorities countered that many of those arguing for the state had been Tilghman's friends and that the victim's popularity would have undue influence on any state trial.

Lynn was held on a federal warrant in the Hughes County jail in Holdenville until his hearing before Commissioner Crutcher on November 8. The prosecution — Assistant State Attorney General Edwin Dabney and Hughes County attorney Walter S. Billingsley — asked that Lynn be held without bond, but Crutcher set bail at $10,000, which Lynn posted ten minutes after adjournment. Almost immediately, the state issued its own warrant only to have federal judge F. E. Kennamer, a friend of Lynn, order an injunction on November 10 preventing Seminole County Sheriff J. A. Doyle from arresting Lynn, who was soon free to travel throughout the state on a writ of habeas corpus.

Wewoka, Oklahoma — site of the trial of Wiley Lynn for the murder of Bill Tilghman — as it appeared in the 1920s. (Archives & Manuscripts Division of the Oklahoma Historical Society, Photo Number 19076.33)

The state-vs.-federal debate was settled at federal court early the next year. Kennamer recused himself, citing his friendship with Lynn, and was replaced by Judge Arba S. Van Valkenberg of Kansas City. Arguments were heard January 7 in Tulsa, when the state won jurisdiction and Lynn's habeas corpus writ was dissolved. Although Lynn's attorneys were given thirty days to appeal, no action was taken, possibly because of some undisclosed sickness (whether of Lynn or his lawyers is not clear), and on February 23 Lynn surrendered to Doyle.

The district judge for Hughes and Seminole Counties was George C. Crump, but he recused himself on April 27 and was replaced by Twenty-fifth District Judge Frank Matthews.

Defending Lynn would be W. W. Pryor of Holdenville and W. M. Stokes of Wewoka, both apparently part of the Pryor, Stokes and Carver firm in Wewoka, and C. A. Sneed of Madill. The prosecution team consisted of Billingsley, Dabney, Roy Hoffman of Oklahoma City, and Price Freeling, a former attorney general appointed special prosecutor for the case.

On Thursday, May 21, 1925, after motions by Lynn's lawyers to quash and a demurrer were overruled, the trial began in Wewoka. Inside the packed courtroom sat widow Zoe Tilghman and Wiley Lynn's father from Madill. *Voir dire* was expected to take two days, but by noon, a tentative jury had been selected.

Lynn's counsel asked each veniremen: "If it should develop that the trial of this tragedy leads from the state capital like a red ribbon down into the town of Cromwell, would that prejudice you in any way?"[5]

Two peremptory challenges were made by the state, while the defense exercised three. Transcripts have not survived, but the jury included Indian minister Houston Miller, merchant Ben Edwards, hardware dealer Troy Robinson, grocer C. W. (or G. W.) Cohea, and farmers C. A. Thomas, W. T. Hale, F. R. Miller, and W. F. Shepherd. As far as the remaining four jurors are concerned, the *Daily Oklahoman* listed farmer D. A. Sandlin, mill and feed dealer Jim McUnder, and Ira Reed and T. A. Bent, whose occupations were not listed; while the *Tulsa Tribune* named merchant Ben Edwards, grocer Dan Settles, banker L. W. Corartm, and farmer J. H. Funston.

The state, jurors were informed, would be seeking the death penalty.

The trial drew media attention across the state. The *Ardmore Daily Press* reported:

Carl Holden and Con Kiersey will leave today for Wewoka, where they will testify in the trial of Wiley Lynn, who is charged with the murder of William Tilghman, veteran peace officer, at Cromwell. The local officers will testify for the defense at this trial. The local officers say that they came in contact with Lynn on many occasions when the defendant was a deputy sheriff in Marshall county and they state that he never drank to their knowledge.

The local officers probably will be called as character witnesses in this trial. Mr. Kiersey and Mr. Holden were at Cromwell two days previous to the shooting of Tilghman by Lynn.

At the time Wiley Lynn is being tried for murder in Wewoka, his cousin, Ernest Lynn of Marshall county will be tried at Sherman, Texas, for violation of the Dyer Act, which is a government enactment governing the cases where stolen automobiles are transferred from one state to another.

Together with Lynn a number of Marshall and Johnston county men have been indicted for violating the Dyer Act, the Ford dealer at Tishomingo being one of those under indictment.[6]

On one hand, Tilghman was called a "pioneer peace officer" and "one of the last of Oklahoma's early day officers," while Lynn was painted as a drunken corrupt lawman. The state wanted to show that Lynn had been drinking and did not act in good faith when he went to raid Murphy's. The defense planned to show that Lynn went to Cromwell after hearing that narcotics and whiskey were kept in the dance hall, and that he shot Tilghman when the latter tried to disarm him. Not all newspapers, however, painted Tilghman as a saint. The *Wewoka Capital-Democrat* said:

> The case has attracted wide attention due to the fact that Tilghman was said to be a notorious character....He had killed numbers of men, so reports say, and featured his activities in a five-reel motion picture production that has been shown in most every city and hamlet in the state. Tilghman planned an additional two-reel picture showing Cromwell as it was in October and November of 1924, featuring Murphy's dance hall, Judge Crump's famous chain-gang, and his suppression of lawlessness and vice there.[7]

On the other hand, the *Capital-Democrat* reported, Lynn "is known throughout this section of the state as a fearless, courageous, enforcement officer. It is said that Lynn dealt misery to the man who attempted to manufacture whiskey in this section of the state and had brought about the conviction of a large number of law violators."[8]

The courtroom showdown promised to be scandalous, and it lived up to its billing on Friday, May 22.

In opening statements, Price Freeling said the state would show that Lynn fired his pistol "to see if it would work" and met Tilghman on the steps to the dance hall. With his own gun drawn but held upright, Tilghman told Lynn to stop and took the pistol from Lynn, who drew a second weapon with his left hand and shot and killed the veteran lawman.

W. W. Pryor made the defense's opening argument, lacerating Tilghman as being sent to Cromwell by Governor Trapp despite protests from Seminole County authorities. Lynn's weapon was fired accidentally, Pryor argued, not "to see if it would work," and Tilghman stormed outside and aimed his gun at Lynn, not holding it upright.

"Don't, Uncle Bill," Lynn said, "this is Lynn." Tilghman replied, "I don't care who it is. I have you where I want you and am going to kill you."[9] Tilghman then fired his weapon, backed Lynn against the wall, "and started to throttle him."[10] That's when Lynn drew his backup weapon and killed Tilghman.

Instead of being the stand-up peace officer, Tilghman was, the Wewoka attorney said, a bootlegger himself who once took three gallons of booze from a federal officer, sold it, and, after being asked what had become of the contraband, offered to divide the money from the sale. Tilghman wanted to give Cromwell a bad reputation, Pryor said, because he could add another chapter to his movies about lawless Oklahoma.

And what of the passengers, including two women, who arrived in the car with Lynn that night?

Rose Lutke was there, Pryor explained, to search women who were arrested for possession of liquor. Pryor didn't offer the reason Sergeant Thompson and Eva Caton came along. The prosecution, however, said all three passengers had been drinking that night, with the whiskey supplied by Lynn. "Eva Catrom [sic] was almost beyond control, Sargent Thompson was in a bad way and Rose Lutke and Lynn had been drinking," Freeling said. He declared that Lynn shouted profanity at the occupants of a passing motor car.[11]

After Lynn shot Tilghman, Lutke, who "did not bear a good reputation," according to Freeling, asked, "Honey, why did you do that?" Lynn told her to "shut up," and drove away.[12]

When witnesses took the stand for the prosecution, Sergeant Thompson described the journey from Wewoka to Cromwell, saying he had been drinking but wasn't drunk. Next, a former oilfield worker named John R. Striff, said he heard Lynn yell for people to get out of his way, sometimes using offensive language, as he drove toward Cromwell. Striff said he saw Lynn fire his weapon but only later learned that the shots killed Tilghman.

In the packed courtroom, Zoe Tilghman sobbed softly during the session, while Lynn sat impassively near his wife, seventeen-year-old son, and father. "Lynn and Mrs. Tilghman paid scant attention to each other," the *Tulsa Tribune* observed.[13]

In an odd aside, Judge Matthews also took time to warn the jurors about their eating habits. "This is going to be a long drawn out case at best and I don't want any of you getting sick in the middle of it," he said. "Most of you are not used to eating fresh meat and I advise you to eat very little of it, if any. At nearly all cases some member of the jury gets sick and I believe it is from this cause."[14]

The first scandal happened when court recessed for lunch. After the jury left, Matthews ordered Sheriff Doyle to search Lynn. Lynn's son was examined first, but nothing was found on him. When Doyle moved to the defendant, Lynn stood and placed a fully loaded, pearl-handled, silver-plated automatic on the table. Pryor lamely argued that Lynn had been told to bring the pistol, which might be used in evidence. Fully loaded? Matthews didn't buy it, saying Lynn had no right to possess the weapon in court. The state wanted the right to inform the jury of the discovery, but Matthews refused to make a ruling one way or the other (apparently the disclosure was not made).

The state rested Friday afternoon, and the defense began its phase that night. Things didn't go well at all. Judge Matthews refused to allow about twenty defense witnesses to testify, and he scolded Pryor twice when he tried to introduce testimony that Tilghman was corrupt. "I thought you were too good a lawyer to try to introduce this kind of testimony," Matthews told Pryor after the jury had been removed. "You must think you can prove to me the moon is made of green cheese. Even if you could prove all of this it wouldn't justify Lynn for killing Tilghman."[15]

Sheriff Doyle, who had earlier testified for the prosecution, was recalled as a defense witness and asked if Tilghman improved the conditions in Cromwell or caused only strife. Matthews disallowed the line of questioning and instructed the jury to disregard Doyle's answers. He also ruled out testimony by dance-hall girl Marcell Tucker and J. H. Morgan, who ran a drink stand at Cromwell. Morgan had testified that after Lynn arrested his son, Tilghman offered to make a fix.

A widow named Mrs. B. A. Williams said Tilghman told her to make no investments in a Cromwell building "till we get rid of Wylie Lynn." Tilghman also told her, "We are going to skid Mr. Lynn over."[16] Again, Matthews ruled the testimony inadmissible.

By the end of the first day of testimony, the jury had been instructed to disregard all statements from every defense witnesses examined.

Lynn's fortunes improved, however, when trial resumed Saturday.

A week before the shooting, Con Kersey (or Kiersey), a Carter County sheriff's deputy, had arrived in Seminole

County to take a prisoner to Ardmore when he spoke to Tilghman.

"I asked Tilghman how he was getting along," Kersey said, "and he replied: 'I'm getting along fairly well if they didn't keep things shut up. There's a federal officer at Holdenville named Lynn. If I could get rid of him things would go all right. I'm too old to have a young fellow like that try to run me. If he doesn't quit fooling around [with] me I'm going to get shut of him.'"[17]

Kersey said he informed Lynn of Tilghman's statement, and, surprisingly, Judge Matthews allowed the testimony.

The defense continued to score points.

A gum-chewing Rose Lutke testified that Lynn's pistol fired after he got out of the car, and that Tilghman arrived and asked, "What the hell is going on here?" Lynn replied, "Uncle Bill, this is Lynn," but Tilghman stuck his gun barrel in Lynn's ribs and grabbed him by the throat, forcing him against the wall. That's when Lynn shot Tilghman three times.

Under cross-examination by Freeling, however, Lutke said she could not tell if the first shot had been accidental. Although she said she came to search women for contraband liquor, she admitted that she did not know Lynn had planned on raiding the dance hall. She denied ever telling Assistant State Attorney General Edwin Dabney that she had been drinking that night.

U.S. Commissioner Park Crutcher and Hughes County Sheriff Sam Turner took the stand to say that Lynn did not appear to have been drinking that night. Pryor also refuted prosecution witness David Thompson's testimony when he read the Fort Sill sergeant's testimony during the habeas corpus proceedings in January in which Thompson said Lynn and his entourage had made no stops to pick up booze.

Sheriff's Deputy W. I. Aldridge rebutted state witness W. M. Curtis's testimony. On Friday Curtis said he had seen Lynn shoot Tilghman, but Aldridge testified that Curtis did not arrive at the scene until ten minutes after the shooting. The case took another twist when Fate Sanders, a private detective with Oklahoma City's Western Detective Agency, took the stand. Sanders said he had been sent to Cromwell to serve as Tilghman's assistant, earning $10 a day.

"I received my orders from my headquarters after Parker La Moore, secretary to Governor Trapp, made the deal to send me to Cromwell....

"My orders were to help regulate vice conditions in the town. When I arrived there I talked to Tilghman and he told me that Lynn would have to get out of town.

"He said that Lynn was an Arkansas — (profane) — and if he got in the way he would kill him."[18]

It was Sanders's testimony that prompted Governor Trapp to disavow any knowledge of sending Tilghman to Cromwell with the state's blessing.

Late Saturday, Lynn took the stand.

"I drove to Cromwell from Okemah where I had been on business," Lynn testified. "I discovered the hammer of my revolver was drawn back and after getting out of my car I drew the gun to release the hammer. It accidently discharged into the street."[19] Lynn said his right hand had been crippled in a threshing machine accident that cut off his right index finger and rendered his right thumb and middle finger inflexible, so he always fired his weapon left-handed.

Lynn denied that he had been drinking. Although admitting that Sergeant Thompson had picked up a quart of whiskey, Lynn said he smashed the bottle against the car's running board.

For fifty minutes Lynn, speaking steadily, explained his version of the events of the night of November 1, 1924.

Gun in hand, Tilghman approached Lynn after the accidental discharge, saying, "Now I've got you where I want you." Lynn went on: "Tilghman pushed his gun into my side. I grabbed the hammer on his gun so it couldn't be discharged. Hugh Sawyer rushed up and knocked my gun out of my hand."[20]

The jury listened intently as Lynn re-enacted the shooting, using Tilghman's pistol — unloaded — as a prop. While Sawyer tried to help his friend Tilghman, Lynn grabbed the automatic pistol Tilghman held. The gun went off, and Lynn reached with his left hand, drew his other weapon, and fired three times. Two bullets struck the old man while the third shot went wild.

"It was gunplay of high order," the *Daily Oklahoman* reported, "and the courtroom looked on in interested silence."[21]

Edwin Dabney handled the cross-examination, posing as Tilghman as Lynn re-enacted the shooting. Lynn remained calm during the heated interrogation by the prosecutor and held his own.

The state called at least one rebuttal witness. J. W. Williams of Okemah said Lynn had been drinking that day. Lynn's attorneys wanted to refute Williams's testimony but could find no witnesses, so the defense rested at 5 p.m.

After a quiet Sunday, on Monday, May 25, the trial went to the jury. Lynn arrived that morning with his family, laughing. Zoe Tilghman showed up with her three young sons.

In closing arguments, W. A. Billingsley said: "We find hellish liquor in the possession of this officer who was supposed to stamp it out of the county. We find him putting on parties with painted-faced women."[22] Roy Hoffman was even less kind, calling Lutke a "vamp" and criticizing her gum-chewing while testifying.[23]

Billingsley also assailed Fate Sanders, saying, "I would hate awfully bad to be bound by what any detective would say. I don't know a single detective I would believe under oath." That, however, prompted an unidentified defense counsel to shout out, "What about Gordon?", referring to Oscar Gordon, a "state evidence man" who had helped with the prosecution's preparation. Billingsley replied: "Gordon is not a detective."[24]

Regarding Park Crutcher's statement that Lynn had not been drinking, Billingsley said: "Crutcher couldn't tell whether he was drinking or not; he couldn't smell his breath because — well, I won't say that."[25]

Zoe Tilghman cried as Billingsley described her husband's final moments. "Bill, Bill," she said, sobbing.[26]

During the defense's closing, Lynn's counsel asked why the state had not seen fit to put Hugh Sawyer, who had been the closest to the shooting, on the stand.

Judge Matthews's instructions were simple. If the jury believed Lynn shot Tilghman in self-defense, it must acquit. If, however, it found that Lynn had shot Tilghman in premeditated fashion, firing his gun first to draw the old man outside, it must find him guilty.

After four hours of deliberation, the jury was sequestered at 9:35 p.m. Monday. Deliberations would resume at 7:30 a.m. Tuesday.

Meanwhile, Lynn told reporters he expected to be acquitted, either by the jury, or if the trial ended in a hung jury, acquittal if the case went federal. "I haven't a sore spot against anyone," he said."[27]

On Tuesday, May 26, on the jury's fifth ballot, the unanimous verdict was reached at 10:45 a.m.

"Wiley Lynn, federal enforcement officer, was acquitted by a Seminole county jury at 10:40 for the murder of Bill Tilghman, after one of the hardest fought murder trials ever held in the state," the *Wewoka Capital-Journal* reported.[28]

The courtroom fell silent after the verdict was announced.

One juror told the *Tulsa Tribune* that Monday's first ballot had been deadlocked, and by the final vote that night the count stood at seven-to-five for conviction. On Tuesday morning's first ballot, however, the vote was ten-to-two for acquittal. One vote later, it was eleven-to-one for acquittal, after which the lone dissenter agreed to free Wiley Lynn.

After Matthews dismissed the jury, Lynn walked outside to be surrounded by family and friends. No one in the courtroom shook hands.

Aftermath

In a statement after his acquittal, Wiley Lynn said: "I have tried to fight a clean fight and have endeavored not to introduce evidence tending to blacken the character of Uncle Bill or anyone else. I could have cleared myself at Tulsa if I had wanted to drag in others. I have respected the family and I tried to spare them."[29]

Lynn, who had been suspended after Tilghman's death, said he planned on returning to federal work.

Not so fast, ruled Judge Matthews, who hadn't forgotten Lynn's gun-carrying incident in his courtroom. Shortly after Lynn's acquittal for murder, Matthews found him guilty of contempt of court and sentenced him to ninety days in jail. "[T]he court cannot conceive a man so bold, so insolent, so foolish," Matthews said. When Pryor tried to take responsibility, the judge went on: "I can only accept the statement of the counsel with a great deal of reservation. Even if the counsel did advise the defendant to bring the gun into court that will not excuse or extenuate the circumstance."[30]

Lynn was given ninety days to appeal and was freed on a $1,000 bond, although he was later rearrested.

Wiley Lynn did not return to federal law enforcement but instead resigned for undisclosed reasons on July 23, 1925. In her book *Marshal of the Last Frontier: Life and Services of William Matthew (Bill) Tilghman for 50 Years One of the Greatest Peace Officers of the West*, Zoe Tilghman claimed that Lynn was arrested many times after his acquittal, but historian Nancy B. Samuelson verified only a few arrests, ranging from drunkenness to rioting.

As Lynn's spiral continued, the Bill Tilghman story took another strange turn when threats were made against Lynn's life. Tilghman's son William escaped from a Tennessee prison in 1929 and headed for Oklahoma, allegedly planning to kill Lynn, but he was arrested at a bus stop in Davenport, Oklahoma.

Meanwhile, Lynn had been feuding with a man named Crockett Long since their days as deputies, and the bad blood continued, not helped by Lynn's drinking.

On July 17, 1932, Lynn walked into a Madill drugstore and confronted Long, a former police chief working for the State Bureau of Investigation. The two men drew their weapons and started shooting. Long, who had shunned his bulletproof vest because of the heat, was hit with a .38-caliber bullet and fell, but he managed to put four .44 slugs into Lynn with his Smith & Wesson. Two unlucky men were also hit in the exchange. Twenty-two-year-old Rody Watkins was killed, while John R. Hilburn, a catcher for the Kingston baseball team, was shot through his knee, ending his baseball career.

Lynn walked outside, handed his gun to a bystander, and sat on the curb, saying he would not die until he knew for certain that Long was dead. Two hours later Long died, and early the next morning, Wiley Lynn, the man who killed Bill Tilghman, died in the Ardmore hospital.

In the final analysis, neither Wiley Lynn nor Bill Tilghman wore halos. It remains unclear whether Lynn murdered Tilghman or if the shooting was accidental or in self-defense — Lynn always claimed that he did not want to kill "Uncle Bill." What changed the mind of the jurors, who early seemed headed for conviction? That's another mystery. And why didn't the state call Hugh Sawyer to testify? The state did not meet its burden of proof, and acquittal seems the right choice, although — considering Lynn's final years — there's plenty of room for debate. Thanks to Zoe Tilghman's version of history, however, and subsequent works by a variety of writers, including the late Glenn Shirley, Bill Tilghman endures as a monument to law enforcement.

And what of Cromwell, the "wickedest city in the world"?

Oil towns came and went in the Roaring Twenties, and such was the case of Cromwell, although it's still around. The town that had been born in October 1923 and drew thousands of residents within months saw its population decline to 249 by 1930. Whether Bill Tilghman (or perhaps Wiley Lynn) had helped rid Cromwell of its lawless element, the town had a new look even before Lynn was acquitted. As the *Tulsa Tribune* reported on May 26, 1925:

> Cromwell today is a much quieter village than it was last November 1, when Bill Tilghman was shot down while serving as peace officer.
>
> Cromwell was living as a replica of the early frontier days then. Now the Murphy dance hall, in front of which the veteran peace officer was "beaten to the draw," has moved into a livelier section of the oil fields, Struggleville, a few miles north of here.[31]

Chapter Notes

Primary sources: *Shoot from the Lip: The Lives, Legends, and Lies of the Three Guardsmen of Oklahoma and U.S. Marshal Nix* (Shooting Star Press, 1998) by Nancy B. Samuelson; *Ghost Towns of Oklahoma* (University of Oklahoma Press, 1978) by John W. Norris; *Guardian of the Law: The Life and Times of William Matthew Tilghman* (Eakin Press, 1988) by Glenn Shirley; *Marshal of the Last Frontier: Life and Services of William Matthew (Bill) Tilghman for 50 Years One of the Greatest Peace Officers of the West* (Arthur H. Clark Co., 1949) by Zoe A. Tilghman; and various 1924-25 editions of the *Ardmore Daily Press, Ardmore Statesman, Cromwell News, Daily Oklahoman, Tulsa Tribune,* and *Wewoka Capital-Democrat.*

1. *Dodge City Times*, January 4, 1878.
2. *Oklahoma Leader*, July 20, 1916.
3. *Cromwell News*, September 12, 1924.
4. *Ardmore Statesman*, November 16, 1924.
5. *Daily Oklahoman*, May 22, 1925.
6. *Ardmore Daily Press*, May 21, 1925.

7. *Wewoka Capital-Democrat*, May 21, 1925.

8. Ibid.

9. *Tulsa Tribune*, May 22, 1925.

10. Ibid.

11. Ibid.

12. Ibid.

13. Ibid.

14. Ibid.

15. *Daily Oklahoman*, May 23, 1925.

16. Ibid.

17. *Tulsa Tribune*, May 23, 1925.

18. *Tulsa Tribune*, May 24, 1925.

19. Ibid.

20. Ibid.

21. *Daily Oklahoman*, May 24, 1925.

22. *Tulsa Tribune*, May 25, 1925.

23. *Wewoka Capital-Democrat*, May 28, 1925.

24. *Tulsa Tribune*, May 25, 1925.

25. Ibid.

26. *Wewoka Capital-Democrat*, May 28, 1925.

27. *Daily Oklahoman*, May 26, 1925.

28. *Wewoka Capital-Journal*, May 28, 1925.

29. *Tulsa Tribune*, May 26, 1925.

30. *Daily Oklahoman*, May 27, 1925.

31. *Tulsa Tribune*, May 26, 1925.

Bibliography

Internet

Alfred Packer,
http://www.archives.state.co.us/packer.html#inventory

"Alfred, or Alferd? and Other Packer Questions" by Ed Quillen, *Colorado Central Magazine*, September 1995, Page 22
http://www.cozine.com/archive/cc1995/00190226.htm

The Handbook of Texas Online, www.tsha.utexas.edu/handbook/online

"Historic Listings of National Park Service Officials,"
www.cr.nps.gov/history/online_books/tolson/histlist7y.htm

Lake City, Colorado: A National Historic Mining District,
www.sangres.com/lakecity.htm

Lake City, Colorado — A Short History,
www.narrowgauge.org/ncmap/excursion7_lake_city.html

Modoc War — The Trial of Captain Jack, www.education.opb.org/learning/opg/modoc/trial.html

"Thomas Cruse, Brigadier General, United States Army,"
www.arlingtoncemetery.com/tcruse.htm

Trial of Oliver Lee, www.htg-is.vianet.nct/~artphe/olee/htm

"Will Croft Barnes and the Apache Uprising of 1881: Adventures of a Soldier and Versatile Citizen of the Southwest" by Paul J. Scheips, www.usaic.hua.army.mil/History/Html/schieps.html

"William Harding Carter, Major General, United States Army,"
www.arlingtoncemetery.com/whcarter.htm

"The Long Trail That Ended in Cromwell: The Life and Death of Legendary Lawman Bill Tilghman" by G. Wayne Tilman, July 1999, www.billtilghman.org

Letters

Ken Hodgson, Fort Davis, Texas, to Johnny D. Boggs, Santa Fe, New Mexico, August 30, 2001, via e-mail.

Margaret B. Finnerty, Saguache County Museum, Saguache, Colorado, to Johnny D. Boggs, Santa Fe, New Mexico, February 15, 2002, via e-mail.

Government, Archival, and Miscellaneous Documents

Alfred Packer Collection, Colorado State Archives

Annual Report of the Commissioner of Indian Affairs to the Secretary of the Department of Interior for the Year 1881, Report of the Commissioner of Indian Affairs, October 24, 1881, National Archives.

Christensen, Eugene. "The Trial and Execution of Jack McCall," December 1948, South Dakota Collection, Carnegie Library, Yankton, South Dakota.

Comanche County District Clerk Holdings (John Wesley Hardin indictment, charge of grand jury foreman, certificate of prison conduct, DeWitt County Sheriff's Office letter to Colonel Buck Waltin. The letter and certificate are reproductions from the Texas State Archives holdings).

Cruz Richards Alvarez memoir, American Life Histories, Federal Writers' Project, 1936-1940.

Eldero Chavez memoir, American Life Histories, Federal Writers' Project, 1936-1940.

T. N. McKinney memoir, American Life Histories, Federal Writers' Project, 1936-1940.

Records of the Judge Advocate General's Office, RG 153, Court-Martial Case Files, Trial of Enlisted Men at Fort Grant, Arizona Territory, 1881, National Archives.

The United States versus John McCall, alias Jack McCall. Trial documents, 1876-1877, Federal Records Center, National Archives-Central Plains Region.

War with the Modoc Indians, 1872-1873; 43rd Congress, 1st Session; House of Representatives Executive Document No. 122; 1874, New Mexico State Library, Serial Set Volume 1607.

Newspapers

Albuquerque Daily Citizen

Albuquerque Journal

Ardmore Daily Press

Ardmore Statesman

Arizona Daily Star

Army and Navy Journal

Austin Statesman

Bellows Falls Times

Black Hills Daily Times

Black Hills Pioneer

Black Hills Weekly

Chicago Times

Cromwell News

Daily Journal

Daily Oklahoman

Dakota Herald

Dallas Daily Herald

Dallas Weekly Herald

Dallas Morning News

Denver Post

Denver Republican

Denver Sunday Times

Denver Times

Dodge City Times

El Paso Daily Herald

El Paso Herald-Post

El Paso Times

Fort Worth Record

Galveston Daily News

Galveston Weekly News

Georgetown Courier

Globe Live Stock Journal

Harper's Weekly

Houston Chronicle

Lake City Silver World

Lead Daily Call

Littleton Independent

Missouri Republican

New York Herald

New York Times

Oklahoma City Times

Oklahoma Leader

Orange County Register

Rio Grande Republican

Rocky Mountain News

Saguache Chronicle

St. Louis Daily Globe-Democrat

San Francisco Daily Morning Call

Santa Fe Daily New Mexican

Sioux City Journal

Tulsa Tribune

Victoria Advocate

Austin Weekly Democratic Statesman

Wewoka Capital-Democrat

Yankton Press and Dakotaian

Magazine Articles

Bankes, James. "'Wild Bill' Hickok," *Wild West*, August 1996.

Boggs, Johnny D., "Famous Frontiersmen Onstage," *The Elks Magazine*, April 2001.

____, "Guns of the West: The Texas-Made Dance Revolver Was the Confederate Version of the Popular, Union-Made Colt," *Wild West*, December 2000.

Brinckerhoff, Sidney B. "Aftermath of Cibecue: Court Martial of the Apache Scouts, 1881," *The Smoke Signal*, No. 36, Fall 1978.

Deac, Wilfred P. "War without Heroes," *Wild West*, April 1991.

Harte, John Bret, "The Strange Case of Joseph C. Tiffany: Indian Agent in Disgrace," *Journal of Arizona History*, No. 16, Vol. 4, Winter 1975.

Metz, Leon C. "John Wesley Hardin and His Women," *Wild West*, April 1999.

____. "Billy the Kid and Pat Garrett," *True West*, July 1997.

____. "Strange Death of Pat Garrett," *Wild West*, February 1998.

____. "*True West* Legends: John Selman," *True West*, May 1998.

____. "*True West* Legends: Pat Garrett," *True West*, July 1997.

Miller, Rick. "Boastful Bill Longley: Cold-Blooded Texas Killer," *Wild West*, February 2002.

Rhodes, L. Patschke. "Wild Bill Longley," *Old West*, Winter 1965.

Riddle, Pax. "Warriors and Chiefs: Winema, a Modoc woman, stood boldly before Captain Jack's warriors. 'Go ahead and shoot me,' she said, but she quickly added that she would shoot one of them first." *Wild West*, April 1999.

Rosa, Joseph G. "From Troy Grove to the Tin Star," *True West*, August/September 2001.

_____. "Wild Bill: Prince of the Pistoleers," *True West*, August/September 2001.

Sorg, Eric V. "Why Buffalo Bill's Wild West," *Old West*, Spring 1997.

Sullivan, Freyda. "An Army Doctor in the Far West Part II — Pacific Shores," *The Tombstone Epitaph*, December 2001.

"A Trip to the Black Hills," *Scribner's Monthly*, April 1877.

Turner, Thadd. "Location, Location, Location: New Evidence Reveals the True Location of the Trial of Jack McCall," *True West*, August/September 2001.

Wolfe, Eugene. "Gunfighters & Lawmen: In 1870, James Butler Hickok invested his gambling winnings in his own Wild West show — with no less dicey results," *Wild West*, October 1994.

Worcester, Don. "Apache Ghost Dance," *Wild West,* August 1995.

_____. "Apache Scouts and Pack Trains," *True West*, February 1996.

Wukovits, John F. "Gunfighters & Lawmen: John Wesley Hardin unknowingly scripted his own epitaph," *Wild West*, June 1990.

Books

Adams, Ramon F. *Western Words: A Dictionary of the American West.* Norman: University of Oklahoma Press, 1968.

Ball, Eve. *Indeh: An Apache Odyssey.* Norman: University of Oklahoma Press, 1988.

Bartholomew, Ed. *Wild Bill Longley: A Texas Hard-Case.* Austin: Nortex Press, 1986.

Basso, Keith H. *The Cibecue Apache.* New York: Holt, Rinehart and Winston, 1970.

Bennett, Granville G. *Reports of Cases Argued and Determined in the Supreme Court of the Territory of Dakota from its Organization to and including the December Term, 1877.* Yankton: Bowen & Kingsbury, Law Publishers, 1879.

Bourke, John G. *Apache Medicine-Men.* New York: Dover Publications, 1993. Reprint of "The Medicine-Men of the Apache,"

Ninth Annual Report of the Bureau of Ethnology to the Secretary of the Smithsonian Institution, 1887-'88, 1892.

____. *On the Border with Crook.* New York: Charles Scribner's Sons, 1891.

Breihan, Carl W. *Great Gunfighters of the West.* New York: Signet, 1977.

Brown, Dee. *Bury My Heart at Wounded Knee.* New York: Washington Square Press, 1970, 1981.

Calhoun, Frederick S. *The Lawmen: United States Marshals and Their Deputies, 1789-1989.* Washington and London: Smithsonian Institute Press, 1989.

Collins, Charles. *Apache Nightmare: The Battle at Cibecue Creek.* Norman: University of Oklahoma Press, 1999.

____. *The Great Escape: The Apache Outbreak of 1881.* Tucson: Westernlore Press, 1994.

Crews, D'Anne McAdams, editor. *Huntsville and Walker County, Texas: A Bicentennial History.* Huntsville: Sam Houston State University Press, 1976.

Cruse, Thomas. *Apache Days and After.* Lincoln: University of Nebraska Press, 1987 (Reprint of 1941 Caxton Printers Ltd. edition, Caldwell, Idaho).

Cunningham, Eugene. *Triggernometry: A Gallery of Gunfighters.* Norman: University of Oklahoma Press, 1996.

Dallas, Sandra. *Colorado Ghost Towns and Mining Camps.* Norman: University of Oklahoma Press, 1985.

Davis, Britton. *The Truth about Geronimo.* Lincoln: University of Nebraska Press, 1976.

Emmitt, Robert. *The Last War Trail: The Utes & the Settlement of Colorado.* Boulder: University Press of Colorado, 2000.

Faust, Patricia L., editor. *Historical Times Illustrated Encyclopedia of the Civil War.* New York: Harper and Row, 1986.

Fenwick, Robert W. "Red." *Alfred Packer: The True Story of the Man-Eater.* Gunnison: B&B Printers, 1963.

Frazer, Robert W. *Forts of the West: Military Forts and Presidios and Posts Commonly Called Forts West of the Mississippi River to 1898*. Norman: University of Oklahoma Press, 1965, 1972.

Fulton, Maurice G. *History of the Lincoln County War*. Tucson: University of Arizona Press, 1968.

Gantt, Paul H. *The Case of Alfred Packer The Man-Eater: An Unsolved Mystery of the West*. Denver: University of Denver Press, 1952.

Garrett, Pat, writer, and Nolan, Frederick, editor. *Pat F. Garrett's The Authentic Life of Billy, the Kid: An Annotated Edition*. Norman: University of Oklahoma Press, 2000.

Gibson, A. M. *The Life and Death of Colonel Albert Jennings Fountain*. Norman: University of Oklahoma Press, 1965.

Gillett, James B. *Six Years with the Texas Rangers 1875 to 1881*. Lincoln: University of Nebraska Press, 1976.

Gorzalka, Ann. *Wyoming's Territorial Sheriffs*. Glendo: High Plains Press, 1998.

Grimes, Roy, editor. *300 Years in Victoria County*. Victoria: Victoria Advocate Publishing Company, 1968.

Guns and Ammo. Guns and the Gunfighters. Los Angeles: Petersen Publication Company, 1975.

Hardin, John Wesley. *The Life of John Wesley Hardin as Written by Himself*. Norman: University of Oklahoma Press, 1961.

North Pacific History Company. *History of the Pacific Northwest Oregon and Washington*. Portland: North Pacific History Company, 1889.

Jameson, W. C. *Unsolved Mysteries of the Old West*. Plano: Republic of Texas Press, 1999.

Keleher, William A. *Violence in Lincoln County 1869-1881*. Albuquerque: University of New Mexico Press, 1982.

Knight, Oliver. *Following the Indian Wars: The Story of the Newspaper Correspondents Among the Indian Campaigners*. Norman: University of Oklahoma Press, 1993.

Kuykendall, W. L. *Frontier Days: A True Narrative of Striking Events on the Western Frontier.* No City: J. M. and H. L. Kuykendall, 1917.

Lamar, Howard R., editor. *The New Encyclopedia of the American West.* New Haven: Yale University Press, 1998.

Landrum, Francis S. *Guardhouse, Gallows and Graves: The Trial and Execution of Indian Prisoners of the Modoc Indian War by the U.S. Army 1873.* Klamath Falls: Klamath County Museum, 1988.

Lockwood, Frank C. *The Apache Indians.* Lincoln: University of Nebraska Press, 1987.

Malsch, Brownson. *Indianola: The Mother of Western Texas.* Austin: State House Press, 1988.

Masterson, William Barclay "Bat." *Gunfighters of the Western Frontier.* Austin: Proofmark Publishing (Reprint of 1907, 1908 publication).

McClintock, John S. *Pioneer Days in the Black Hills: Accurate History and Facts Related By One of the Early Day Pioneers.* Norman: University of Oklahoma Press, 2000.

Metz, Leon C. *John Wesley Hardin: Dark Angel of Texas.* Norman: University of Oklahoma Press, 1996.

_____. *Pat Garrett: The Story of a Western Lawman.* Norman: University of Oklahoma Press, 1974.

Miller, Nyle H., and Snell, Joseph W. *Great Gunfighters of the Kansas Cowtowns, 1867-1886.* Lincoln: University of Nebraska Press, 1967.

Miller, Rick. *Bloody Bill Longley.* Wolfe City: Henington Publishing Company, 1996.

Monnett, John H. *Tell Them We Are Going Home: The Odyssey of the Northern Cheyennes.* Norman: University of Oklahoma Press, 2001.

Morris, John W. *Ghost Towns of Oklahoma.* Norman: University of Oklahoma Press, 1978.

Murray, Keith A. *The Modocs and Their War*. Norman: University of Oklahoma Press, 1959.

Nevin, David. *The Soldiers*. New York: Time-Life Books, 1974.

Nolan, Federick. *The West of Billy the Kid*. Norman: University of Oklahoma Press, 1998.

O'Connor, Richard. *Wild Bill Hickok*. New York: Konecky & Konecky, 1987.

O'Neal, Bill. *Fighting Men of the Indian Wars*. Stillwater: Barbed Wire Press, 1991.

Parsons, Chuck and Marjorie. *Bowen and Hardin*. College Station: Creative Publishing Co., 1991.

Quinn, Arthur. *Hell with the Fire Out: A History of the Modoc War*. Boston: Faber and Faber, 1997.

Riddle, Jeff C. *The Indian History of the Modoc War*. Eugene: Urion Press, 1974 (Reprint of the 1914 first edition).

Roberts, David. *Once They Moved Like the Wind: Cochise, Geronimo and the Apache Wars*. New York: Simon and Schuster, 1993.

Rosa, Joseph G. *Age of the Gunfighter*. London: Salamander Books, 1993, 2000.

_____. *Alias Jack McCall: A Pardon or Death*. Kansas City: Kansas City Posse of the Westerners, 1967.

_____. *They Called Him Wild Bill. The Life and Adventures of James Butler Hickok*. Norman: University of Oklahoma Press, 1974.

_____. *The West of Wild Bill Hickok*. Norman: University of Oklahoma Press, 1982.

Schmitt, Martin F., editor. *General George Crook: His Autobiography*. Norman: University of Oklahoma Press, 1946, 1960.

Sherman, James E. and Barbara H. *Ghost Towns and Mining Camps of New Mexico*. Norman: University of Oklahoma Press, 1975.

Shirley, Glenn. *Guardian of the Law: The Life and Times of William Matthew Tilghman*. Austin: Eakin Press, 1988.

Simmons, Virginia McConnell. *The Ute Indians of Utah, Colorado, and New Mexico*. Boulder: University Press of Colorado, 2000.

Sonnichsen, C. L. *Tularosa: Last of the Frontier West*. Albuquerque: University of New Mexico Press, 1960, 1980.

Stamps, Roy & Jo Ann (transcribers and compilers). *The Letters of John Wesley Hardin*. Austin: Eakin Press, 2001.

Straggon, Porter A. *The Territorial Press of New Mexico 1834-1912*. Albuquerque: University of New Mexico Press, 1969.

Tilghman, Zoe A. *Marshal of the Last Frontier: Life and Services of William Matthew (Bill) Tilghman for 50 Years One of the Greatest Peace Officers of the West*. Glendale: Arthur H. Clark Co., 1949.

Trachtman, Paul. *The Gunfighters*. Alexandria: Time-Life Books, 1977.

Tuller, Roger H. *"Let No Guilty Man Escape": A Judicial Biography of "Hanging Judge" Isaac C. Parker*. Norman: University of Oklahoma Press, 2001.

Turner, Thadd. *Wild Bill Hickok: Deadwood City — End of Trail*. Deadwood: Old West Alive! Publishing, 2001.

Tuska, Jon. *Billy the Kid: His Life and Legend*. Albuquerque: University of New Mexico Press, 1994.

Utley, Robert M. *The Indian Frontier of the American West 1848-1890*. Albuquerque: University of New Mexico Press, 1984.

Utley, Robert M. and Washburn, Wilcomb E. *The American Heritage History of the Indian Wars*. New York: American Heritage Publishing/Bonanza Books, 1977.

Wharfield, Colonel H. B. *Cibicu Creek Fight in Arizona: 1881*. El Cajon: Self-published, 1971.

Wiggins, Gary. *Dance & Brothers: Texas Gunmakers of the Confederacy*. Orange, Virginia: Moss Publications, 1986.

Wilkins, Frederick. *The Law Comes to Texas: The Texas Rangers 1870-1891*. Austin: State House Press, 1999.

Index